TEACHING
on
TARGET

TEACHING
on
TARGET

**Models,
Strategies,
and
Methods
That
Work**

Daniel C. Elliott

CORWIN PRESS
A SAGE Publications Company
Thousand Oaks, California

For information:

Corwin Press
A Sage Publications Company
2455 Teller Road
Thousand Oaks, California 91320
www.corwinpress.com

Sage Publications Ltd.
1 Oliver's Yard
55 City Road
London EC1Y 1SP
United Kingdom

Sage Publications India Pvt. Ltd.
B-42, Panchsheel Enclave
Post Box 4109
New Delhi 110 017 India

Printed in the United States of America

Library of Congress Cataloging-in-Publication Data

Elliott, Daniel C.
Teaching on target: Models, strategies, and methods that work / Daniel C. Elliott.
    p. cm.
Includes bibliographical references and index.
ISBN 1-4129-1359-4 (cloth)
ISBN 1-4129-1360-8 (pbk.)
    1. Teaching. 2. Effective teaching. I. Title.
LB1025.3.E43 2005
371.102—dc22

                                        2004024085

This book is printed on acid-free paper.

05   06   07   10   9   8   7   6   5   4   3   2   1

Acquisitions Editor:	Elizabeth Brenkus
Editorial Assistant:	Candice L. Ling
Production Editor:	Denise Santoyo
Copy Editor:	Jackie Tasch
Typesetter:	C&M Digitals (P) Ltd.
Indexer:	Kathy Paparchontis
Cover Designer:	Michael Dubowe
Graphic Designer:	Rose Storey

Contents

List of Figures

Dedication

I became a student of teaching because teaching is what schools are all about. Across my career as an educational leader, I resisted temptations to make schools places of political influence or instances of full employment for less-than-committed government employees. Schools are all about kids being equipped for lifelong success, and teaching is how they become equipped.

I applaud the thousands of enthusiastic teachers whom I have served and encountered, and with whom I shared a mutual joy of teaching. I am grateful to the many who have shared their teaching ideas with me and have helped to develop sample lessons to illustrate these models, methods, and strategies. Every lesson reported herein was a real lesson, done to illustrate the point but also done to discover if the point was worth illustrating. Some of the strategies we developed were not worth the trouble of illustrating to you. They were mediocre at best, and teaching school has *nothing* to do with mediocrity. So we have left some sample lesson development up to you, the creative teacher-reader, seeking to make the best professional decisions about how to serve the needs of the learners before you.

I dedicate this book as a salute to great teachers everywhere who put students first, who love and respect their students enough to invest themselves into preparing for the *best possible outcomes*. I dedicate it to all those teachers who go far beyond union contract work rules and *serve* their learners' needs. I applaud their creativity and commitment. They are professionals and should be recognized as such—the greatest of all professions' professionals—for they make the future possible for young people.

Preface

Throughout recent decades and their cycles of educational reform, the collection of teaching methodologies has been growing. Many teachers have used these methodologies and the models derived from them for many years, perhaps without knowing the names given to them by pedagogues. Excellent teachers discovered that these methodologies were effective in certain situations and, therefore, used them repeatedly. Educational researchers have observed these successful teaching practices, related them to earlier writings in educational research, and given them names, along with synthesized applications and procedures. The focus and purpose of this book is to introduce many of these models, strategies, and methods to new generations of teachers.

To draw an analogy, ancient archers created many different types of arrows to meet various challenges and circumstances. When one type of arrow failed to satisfy the archer's purpose, he or she would craft a different one, better suited to the need. Each arrow had its purpose, whether or not it had a distinctive name. This book can be a quiver for today's excellent teachers. It is not necessarily designed to be read cover to cover as entertainment. Rather, it was created to serve much like the archer's quiver, containing examples of different options among which the expert teacher might select when making the major decisions related to designing classroom learning experiences. The book includes a table of contents and an index to serve in quickly finding information desired so that it might be applied creatively within the teacher's planning process.

Professionally aware teachers may not recognize some of the names and terms described herein, but they will certainly recognize most of the procedures as elements in their commonsense collection of pedagogical arrows, arrayed in the quiver, awaiting the teacher's selection for just the right instructional target.

These models constitute a basic repertoire for schooling. With them, we can accomplish most of the common goals of schools. They also represent a broad range of approaches to education. They reflect many of the major philosophical and psychological orientations toward teaching and learning, including some that are highly controversial and should be used judiciously.

These models have long histories of practice and have been refined through experience. They are adaptable to the learning styles of students and adjustable to subject matter variance. Bruce Joyce and Marsha Weil (2000) have presented deep and insightful research on them for several decades. To help teachers understand how to apply each model directly, four key ideas are presented by which the models may be analyzed and compared.

Describing the Models

1. **The Plan:** The section on the *plan* describes the stages or elements of the model in action. Sequenced activities make up the *elements*. Each model has a distinctive flow of elements.

2. **Structure of the Learning Climate:** The discussion of *necessary structure* describes student and teacher roles and relationships and the norms that are encouraged. It also reveals the degree of structure necessary in the learning environment.

3. **Teacher/Learner Interaction:** *Teacher/learner interaction* suggests how teachers are to regard learners and how they would best respond to what learners do.

4. **Outcomes:** Finally, the section on *outcomes* describes how both instructional and nurturing outcomes are achieved as teachers lead learners in certain directions.

These four concepts can be viewed as a way of communicating the basic procedures involved in implementing any instructional model.

Teaching continues to be viewed as an art, although an increasing scientific knowledge base is developing to support and transmit successful practice. Teachers should see the models of teaching in this book as ways of accomplishing a wide variety of purposes. No single teaching methodology can accomplish every purpose. Wise teachers master a sufficient repertoire of strategies to deal with any specific learning problems they encounter. Preservice teachers might master four or five of the more dependable and accepted models as a beginning repertoire, including one model from each family. Master teachers, of course, will be able to call up and use many more. The most creative educators, however, rarely limit their repertoires to only what exists. They use available models as stimulators to their own creativity, rather than as recipes. In many lessons, faced with the complex needs of many classroom situations, the most effective teachers integrate two or more models.

The terms *model, strategy, method,* and *methodology* are often used interchangeably in discussions of teaching. In this book, however, these terms are used with the following precise meanings.

Some Important Terms

Model: a standardized pattern for lesson organization

Strategy: a particular approach to or application of a given model

> **Method:** a specific application of one or more models blended into a lesson or unit, or a series of lessons or units, targeted to specific students with specific needs
>
> **Methodology:** the collection of teaching methods that a teacher tends to use consistently and repeatedly over time

On the following pages, we consider several models, strategies, and methods of teaching. We begin by setting the stage with standards for effective teaching. These standards are emerging across the country as a formalization of more than 30 years of research about effective teaching and learning. The "effective schools" research, begun back in the 1970s, has been a foundation for all ensuing efforts to reform, restructure, redefine, or recreate the process of teaching and learning in formal public schools across North America.

Effective schooling is not possible without effective classroom management. Classroom management is presented in Chapter 2 as a means of expressing wise, loving, and nurturing care for students in the school. It is not a mere process of manipulating class members but of serving them according to their needs. This section offers students of teaching a number of creative ideas and approaches related to managing flow of activity and the highly important task of holding students to account for their conduct in the classroom.

In Chapter 3, we discuss how to design learning and emphasize the importance of *teaching to an objective* or outcome. The chapter also discusses the roles played by goals, objectives, and activities when planning for teaching. We describe the *General Model for Teaching*, which is designed to include all teaching methods of most teachers in most circumstances.

Chapter 4 introduces the *behavioral models* and a method that integrates several of them:

- Direct instruction
- Mastery learning
- Advance organizer
- Practice theory
- Memory model
- Mastery lecture method

The *information-processing models* make up Chapter 5. These are:

- Concept construction
- Concept attainment
- Synectics

In Chapter 6, several key *inquiry* models are presented:

- Inquiry training
- Scientific inquiry

- Socratic inquiry
- Social science inquiry

The chapter also describes questioning strategies for inquiry teaching. As teachers plan lessons—including their questioning strategies—more thoroughly, their lessons become more successful. We suggest the more thorough planning that teachers can do to prepare the questions they will pose in lessons.

Chapter 7 discusses the *social models*:

- Group investigation
- Cooperative learning
- Peer practice
- Role playing
- Simulations
- Nondirective teaching
- Clarification committees

Chapter 8 discusses the writing process. Types and categories of writing are presented, along with a thorough discussion of holistic scoring of written work. Chapter 9 synthesizes several of the model components and elements into strategies applied to teaching youngsters with special needs. Chapter 10 proceeds to student assessment and grading strategies. The intent of this section is for teachers to develop and understand their *philosophy* for grading and evaluating student work. Chapter 11 helps readers draw all the ideas together, creating something called the *blended model method* and a well-developed plan for instruction.

In many chapters, sample lesson plans are provided, not as lessons to be taken to a classroom and taught, but as examples to show how a model, strategy, or method has been artistically and scientifically applied.

The thrust of this book is to empower you, the creative teacher, to apply these components artfully, as you scientifically go about the process of planning for and delivering instruction to the most important people in the world—the students whose futures have been *entrusted to you*!

Acknowledgments

The author and Corwin Press gratefully acknowledge the contributions of the following individuals:

Jim Carrell, Teacher
Albuquerque Academy, Albuquerque, NM

Susan Cleary, Teacher
Darley Road Elementary School, Claymont, DE

Laura Cumbee, Student Support Teacher
South Central Middle School, Emerson, GA

Gwen E. Gross, Superintendent/Adjunct Professor
Manhattan Beach Unified School District, Manhattan Beach, CA
Pepperdine University, Graduate School of Education, Culver City, CA

Robert Kastelic, Teacher/Adjunct Professor
Northern Arizona University, Flagstaff, AZ

Sharon McClain, Superintendent/Adjunct Faculty Member
Hermosa Beach City School District, Hermosa Beach, CA

Brigid Ovitt, Teacher
Albuquerque Academy, Albuquerque, NM

Linda Purrington, Director, MAETC Program
Graduate School of Education & Psychology, Pepperdine University,
    Los Angeles, CA

Gina Segobiano, Superintendent/Principal
Signal Hill School District No. 181, Belleville, IL

Bonnie Tryon, Principal
2002-2003 NAESP Board of Directors, Golding Elementary School,
    Cobleskill, NY

About the Author

 A native of Southern California, Dan Elliott grew up in a family that struggled to make ends meet. Drawn to the greater cause of making a life different for children trapped by poverty, he began teaching in an elementary school district in 1970 and taught most subjects at each grade from kindergarten through 9th in those early years, many in multiage and looping classroom situations. After completing a master's degree in school administration, he served as a vice principal, principal, central office administrator, small-district superintendent, and county office of education associate superintendent—positions primarily held in his native California. Completion of doctoral studies led him into service as a researcher, speaker, and professor in schools of education since 1991. Dan has taught educational methods and instructional leadership around the world. He is currently a Professor at Azusa Pacific University's School of Education and Behavioral Studies. The contents of his writings reveal a bit of his heart for schools and for the lives of the children that are shaped within those school walls.

Effective Schools and Standards for Teaching

Guiding Questions

1. What are some teacher characteristics for 21st-century teaching?

2. What is it like to be a reflective teacher?

3. How is an attitude of servant-heartedness related to being an effective, accountable teacher?

4. What are the five core propositions from the National Board for Professional Teaching (NBPT)?

5. How might the NBPT propositions and standards help teachers to serve students more effectively?

6. What does diversity have to do with teaching effectiveness?

21ST-CENTURY TEACHING: A NATIONAL MODEL

Although it may be difficult to imagine, there was, in the not-too-distant past, a time and a place where liberals, conservatives, educators, policymakers, and politicians concerned about the preparation of teachers for public schools gathered in a large number to *reason together.* The first national symposium by major teacher educator organizations took place in December 1995. The Association of Teacher Educators, the American Association of Colleges for Teacher Education, and the U.S. Department of Education's Office of Educational Research and Improvement sponsored and conducted a (U.S.) National Congress on Teacher Education. Leading national figures in teacher education presented their views to the almost 500 delegates. Focus groups examined the views and reported to a conference coordinator. The coordinator, in turn, synthesized the concerns, ideas, and recommendations into a daily log of issues. In the end, the group produced a list of desired characteristics for teachers of the 21st century.

Characteristics of 21st-Century Teachers

Hold selfless love for students

Exhibit commitment and fairness to all

Treat students as whole persons

Model thinking and problem-solving strategies

Know students' needs thoroughly

Skillfully manage classroom environments

Lead with global vision and awareness

Manage change positively

Have clear standards and hold high expectations of themselves and others

Work effectively with parents and other adults

The institutions and organizations represented at the congress forged a preliminary national agenda regarding teaching strengths and skills. Effective teachers are reflective, accountable, and most certainly student centered, as opposed to convenience centered or content centered (Elliott, 1996).

Reflective Teachers

The 1995 Congress on Teacher Education described what pupils of the 21st century should be: value minded and caring, understanding of basic human rights, communicators, masters of basic knowledge, information processors, problem solvers, decision makers, and successful at living, among other traits. Such thinking is reminiscent of reflectiveness in teaching practices. Reflectiveness, or thoughtfulness, and the reflection of that thinking onto the learning situation, is an important element for those who would be effective as teachers. More important, it is necessary for those who would be successful as learners and problem solvers. If we are to prepare pupils to become thinking adult citizens, then the teachers must themselves be reflective about their own teaching.

Accountable Teachers

The spectrum of educational spokespersons and inquirers that gathered in Washington, D.C., in 1995 to discover what 21st-century teachers should be like agreed that *teachers must be willing to teach accountably.* Teachers who will be truly effective in their craft will come to understand the importance and the imperative of servanthood. Accountability is a form of servanthood. Servanthood is an attitude that leads one to consider the needs of others and to address those needs. To have the heart of a servant, one is willing to do what might be necessary to discover the need and then to provide a service that will satisfy or fulfill it. Servanthood and servant-heartedness are necessary in skillful teaching. Teachers who see their role in terms of service to others are not distracted by personal considerations, for they see their mission in serving rather than in being served.

Student-Centered Teaching

The thrust of a teacher's efforts must always be to serve students according to their needs. Sometimes, those needs are expressed directly by the learners. However, more often than not, students who may not be able to verbalize the expression of need in specific or accurate terms unconsciously demonstrate those needs. Teachers who center their efforts on the expressed and demonstrated needs of their students, rather than a fixed collection of information or data, have been shown to create far more lasting results, regardless of the subject. The effective teacher's curriculum is not the textbook. Rather, it is the material that the teacher develops with each individual student in mind. What are the individual skills needed? It will not matter that the child arrives without prerequisite skills and abilities. It will remain that teacher's moral duty to teach each child appropriately. When a child's needs are beyond the resources and skills available to a single teacher and classroom, it will yet remain the teacher's duty to facilitate connections so that learning needs may, in the end, be satisfied.

Standards for Teaching: A Holistic Vision

Because of local demand, state reform planning, and national education policies, most states have formally adopted standards for the teaching profession. These are all influenced by the five core propositions developed by the National Board for Professional Teaching (NBPT, 2003). These propositions describe teachers who successfully promote excellence in the students they serve. The following five propositions, sometimes called National Board

Standards, provide patterns for teaching excellence, and we will thread them throughout this book about teaching models, methods, and strategies:

- Teachers are *committed* to students and their learning.
- Teachers *know the subjects* they teach and *how to teach* those subjects to students.
- Teachers are *responsible* for managing and monitoring student learning.
- Teachers *think* systematically about their practice and *learn* from experience.
- Teachers are *members of learning communities.*

Teaching standards often overlap—by design—because they represent a holistic vision emphasizing the complex interrelationships of teaching and learning that exist within 21st-century schools and society. A vision of teaching should emphasize relationships among things like: a teacher's understandings of students; the subject matter and curriculum; and instructional models, methods, and strategies. Each element is tightly linked to how the teacher prepares for each lesson and how the learning outcomes will be assessed.

Of course, teaching is more than mere methodology. Theory and philosophy about teaching and learning must empower reflective teachers to make thoughtful decisions about teaching methods and the support of student learning outcomes. A teacher's practice cannot be viewed or evaluated separately from her or his educational philosophy—professional ideas and understandings about all aspects of teaching.

A Developmental View of Teaching

Teachers' knowledge, skills, and practices develop throughout their professional careers. The nature of teaching requires continuous growth in order to engage and challenge increasingly diverse students in a rapidly changing world. Teachers are never "finished" as professional learners, no matter how extensive or excellent their formal education and preparation. If teachers' expertise, capabilities, and accomplishments are to be enriched over time, the teachers must become reflective practitioners who actively seek to strengthen and augment their professional skills, knowledge, and perspectives throughout their careers. Teachers who think they possess all necessary knowledge and understanding to teach their classes are, to be sure, the least prepared. Effective teachers know that true teaching and learning relationships are based on a mutual journey in which teacher and learner collaborate and both grow.

Individual teachers enter the profession with wide-ranging levels of skills. Because of shortages, many people who now occupy classroom positions have no formal training at all regarding the craft and skill of teaching. It is imperative that all teachers who have attained a professional status of certification are able to deliver the most excellent of teaching practices and assist each other in their journey toward professional practice. New standards for the teaching profession are aimed at producing *professional teachers* who are appropriately equipped.

NATIONAL BOARD FOR PROFESSIONAL TEACHING PROPOSITIONS

1: Teachers are committed to students and their learning.

Effective teachers build on students' prior knowledge, life experience, and interests to achieve learning goals for all students. To do this, teachers use a variety of instructional strategies and resources that respond to students' different needs. They build challenging learning experiences for all their students and create environments that promote autonomy, interaction, and choice. Effective teachers know the importance of actively engaging all students in learning. Doing this requires awareness of every student's needs and abilities. Also, it requires an awareness of problem-solving and critical thinking strategies to use within and across subject matter areas. Concepts and skills are taught in ways that encourage students to apply them in real-life contexts. Thus, effective teachers make subject matter meaningful, assisting all students to become self-directed learners who show, explain, and evaluate their own learning.

Learning will occur when effective teachers strive to help students to see the connections between what they already know and the new material. When teachers assist students to connect classroom learning to their life experiences and cultural understandings, knowledge relationships develop. When students' needs and differences are discerned and all students (including second-language learners) are supported, they achieve learning goals. Effective teachers ponder ways to open a lesson or unit to capture student attention and interest. They build on students' comments and questions during the lesson to extend their understanding. They make "on the spot" changes in the lesson plans based on updated perceptions of students' interests and questions. Last year's lesson plans are not appropriate for today's classrooms where truly effective teachers are concerned.

Effective teachers work to engage *all* students in a variety of learning experiences that accommodate the different ways each learns. Teachers use alternative strategies to introduce, explain, and restate subject matter concepts and processes so that all students understand. They select strategies that make the complexity and depth of subject matter understandable to each learner. Their inclusive strategies support subject matter learning for second-language learners as well. They often modify materials and resources and use appropriate adaptive equipment to support each student's fullest success. Using technology to enhance student learning is familiar stuff for effective teachers. They vary their strategies from hour to hour and day to day. Of course, they recognize whenever a lesson is not working and determine what to do about it.

As teachers develop, they discover ways to use the classroom environment to provide opportunities for independent and collaborative learning. How can a variety of grouping structures be used to promote student interactions and learning? What are the best ways to promote participation and positive interactions between all students? Effective teachers work to support and monitor student autonomy and choice during learning experiences. Effective teachers support and frequently monitor students through extensive collaboration during learning activities. They are quick to help students make decisions about managing time and materials during learning activities.

State and national standards call for teaching effectiveness that provides opportunities for *all* students to think and reflect about their learning, to engage in discussion and interaction, and to evaluate the content and outcomes of their learning. Effective teachers are certain to help *all* students learn through practice and application of subject-specific strategies. They facilitate critical investigation into subject matter concepts and questions by *all* students. *All* students become engaged in problem-solving activities with multiple approaches and solutions. Each learner is encouraged to ask critical questions and consider alternative views. Students are empowered and supported to discover meaning and relationships in learning information presented so that life-forming conclusions can be reached.

In effective classrooms, teachers must plan how to motivate every student to initiate and monitor his or her own learning and to strive for challenging learning goals. Students are encouraged to describe their own learning processes and progress. Teachers are careful to explain clear learning goals for all students for every lesson activity. Students frequently are engaged in chances to consider and assess their own work and that of their peers. Teachers are careful to help all students to create and use personal strategies for knowing about and reflecting on their own learning. Of course, effective teachers help all students, regardless of their prior abilities, to develop and use strategies for accessing knowledge and information related to the current courses of study.

2: Teachers know the subjects they teach and how to teach those subjects to students.

Over the decades, the frustrations often shared by teachers across the nation have been expressed in the plea that people ought to view teachers as much more than baby-sitters or child care workers. But truth is, people still retain these limited views! Teachers and the leaders of schools and school systems have had to change perceptions about the role of teachers. Now, teachers must see themselves as conveyors of real information, transmitted so that it becomes meaningful knowledge in the minds of learners. Successful teachers promote both the understanding of information and the application of it in ways that are productive and meaningful to the learner across time. Creative teachers use the subjects they deliver as access points into the domains of social understanding, cultural relevance, ethical propositions and worldviews, and the operations of our physical world.

Effective teachers are well prepared and exhibit a strong working knowledge of subject matter, as well as of student development. This standard is, perhaps, the central core to *effective teaching*. With our best strategies and our most loving and serving attitudes, we cannot make a difference in the lives of our learners if we have nothing to teach them. To teach anything to others, we must know and understand it well ourselves. Effective teachers are able to organize curriculum in ways that enhance students' understanding of the central themes, concepts, and skills in the subject area. Then, these teachers interrelate such ideas and information within and across the various curricular domains so that student understanding is enriched. By careful and clever use of their understanding of both the learners and the subject, these effective teachers allow the subject matter to become accessible to all of the class members.

Using curriculum guides and frameworks as well as state curriculum standards, effective teachers can identify and understand the key concepts and underlying themes and relationships in the material to be taught. They ensure that the subject matter incorporates diverse perspectives, and they work to keep themselves current in the subjects they teach so that they can adequately support student learning. They are attentive to students' linguistic and cognitive development as well as their physical development.

Effective teachers use their knowledge about human development to organize and sequence the curriculum to increase student understanding. They also accomplish this by investing effort to master subject matter. Because of their subject matter knowledge, they are able to plan units and instructional activities that demonstrate key concepts and their interrelationships. Teachers' efforts to organize subject matter effectively reveal how they value different cultural perspectives. They are consistent as they incorporate subject or grade-level expectations into their planning for student learning outcomes. Thus, they ensure that students develop a deep understanding of core concepts in each subject matter area.

Effective teachers realize that students develop real knowledge through understanding and application linked to the information centered in the instructional objectives and subject content. Many have debated the relative importance of content versus process in modern education, and those debates will likely continue indefinitely. Truth is, both are essential. Effective teachers know the material that must be mastered by students in the educational arena. The teachers are, themselves, true masters of those content areas, as demonstrated by their undergraduate and graduate school preparation for teaching. Then, effective teachers are also equipped with creative and unique methods and strategies for teaching. They design most of these themselves, using basic models and patterns in the educational literature but filtering through the teachers' professional decisions about the actual needs of the actual students sitting in the classroom.

Part of teaching well includes the use of the physical environment to promote learning. Effective teachers who know how to teach their subjects also tend to make creative use of the spaces in which they teach.

When teachers create physical environments that engage all students, they approach teaching effectiveness. They strive to engage each learner in purposeful learning activities and encourage constructive interactions among students. Effective teachers maintain classrooms and learning spaces that are safe, places where fairness and personal respect are the expected and enforced norm and where students assume responsibility for themselves and others. Everyone is moved to participate in the making of appropriate decisions independently and in collaboration with others. Student conduct expectations are clearly understood and consistently maintained. Through intriguing and interesting learning routines and processes, teachers effectively use instructional time.

Effective teachers are quick to arrange their classrooms in ways that inspire positive classroom interactions. Seating is adapted to accommodate individual and group needs. Materials, as well as technology and other learning resources, are easily accessible. The classroom environment reflects and promotes learning performance outcomes by all, and the place is seen as safe for each class member.

A goal that all effective teachers never surrender is the need for each to be respectful toward the others, including those who may be different from them. These teachers model and promote fairness. They demonstrate respect by carefully considering how they approach each individual student. They recognize effort and achievement by every member of the class and reinforce contributions that lead to meaningful learning. They are able to help students take risks and exercise creativity. Effective teachers consistently recognize and respond to inappropriate conduct in ways that are fair and equitable.

Daily classroom activity is designed to assist each individual learner to communicate respect and accept different points of view, discuss and disagree with ideas without condemning individual personhood, and recognize the mutual search for truth in which all are engaged. Students are often organized in groups to promote social development and social understanding. Teachers strive to develop students' self-esteem. They create opportunities for students to work cooperatively toward mutually important goals. They teach students appropriate leadership skills. Classroom procedures and standards are developed to promote individual responsibility and inspire all students toward self-direction in their learning habits.

Effective teachers pay attention to students and strive to understand the reasons for student behavior. The standards of behavior always reflect the learning needs of the class. Teachers are consistent and fair with enforcement and intervene when student behavior does not meet agreed-upon classroom standards. Students are involved in making decisions about classroom procedures. With their management strategies, effective teachers help all students learn to solve problems and resolve conflicts. They help the students to exercise personal responsibility. They are careful to include families in the development, monitoring, and enforcement of personal responsibility for the student.

Daily schedules, time lines, classroom routines, and classroom rules are created in ways that involve *all* the students. Teachers then help students to internalize classroom rules, routines, and procedures so they can become self-directed learners. A climate of fairness and respect is generated by classroom procedures and effective teachers' consistent attitude. Procedures are held as flexible standards and not rigid rules in order to help each student uniquely, equitably, but in fairness to all others.

Daily instruction is the priority in time allotment. Effective teachers develop ways to avoid losing valuable time to activities like taking roll, cleanup, and interruptions. Students are helped to remain on task and attentive to the learning process. Lessons and activities are designed to facilitate efficient transitions from one to another. Often, drill and review is conducted during cleanup and other transition periods. Administrative tasks are addressed in ways that have minimal impact on learning activities.

Standards for teaching clearly reveal that effective teachers in the 21st century are able to vary lesson design according to the diverse needs of class members every time the curriculum is covered. They develop and use a repertoire of instructional strategies suitable for the particular subject matter. But they also use their knowledge of subject matter to help students construct their own knowledge. They can develop interesting instructional strategies that challenge all students to think critically in each subject area. They use students' life experiences, prior knowledge, and interests to make the content relevant and meaningful to them. Their quiverful of diverse strategies and methods draws from a variety of recognized instructional patterns to illustrate various concepts and their connections within and across subject areas. With such creativity, effective teachers help all students to develop enthusiasm for and a deep knowledge of the subject matter.

Emerging technologies are tools that 21st-century effective teachers use invisibly and confidently, along with other materials, to organize and deliver the curriculum. The selected materials and technologies promote students' understanding of subject matter. Teacher planning for instructional materials reflects the diversity in their classrooms. Creative use of technology highlights key concepts in the subject matter. These teachers are careful to help all students gain access to useful materials, resources, and technologies to support their learning.

3: Teachers are responsible for managing and monitoring student learning.

Truly effective teachers are masters of the classroom in which they serve. They are able to attend to all the activities of all of the students because they planned for those very activities and created effective implementation strategies that motivate student involvement, engagement, and productivity. Such teachers attend to the activities of the students and are fully equipped to make formal and informal assessments of student learning. They are always monitoring student growth. Every assignment, every class activity, every sponge activity in between formal lessons is designed with assessment of student growth in mind. The learning environment is created and arranged with learning and outcome assessment in mind. These teachers are able to assess their students individually as well as the progress of small groups or even the whole class as a group.

Teachers deserving of the title care about how well students learn. Therefore, they clearly communicate to all learners the goals for learning. They collect information that illustrates student-learning outcomes. They involve the students in assessing their own learning outcomes. They also use a variety of sources and techniques to measure these outcomes. Effective teachers also are effective communicators with the students' parents about student learning success. They find ways to engage parents in the assessment of learning by monitoring student demonstrations of learning at home. Their assessment strategies go well beyond the standardized test that is the darling of legislators and policy wonks across the nation. They are able to use Individual Education Plans (IEPs), curriculum content standards developed by state departments of education, and personalized assessment tools created by the teacher for each of the students.

Effective teachers find ways to make assessment a fundamental part of all learning processes. They model strategies for assessing the students both collectively and individually. This modeling is done so that students can develop understanding about how and why they may assess their own learning growth; as a result, all students become self-directed learners. Peer discussions and cooperative learning activities teach learners to assess themselves and mentor one another.

Effective teachers use the assessment tools as part of comprehensive planning for instruction that is aimed at growing each learner according to the need to reach potential. Instructional decisions are made on the basis of assessment data rather than personal whim or what the teacher next door is trying. Teaching strategies are selected because of effective student assessment. With this information, effective teachers are able to inform students about their progress and help them to plan for improving their own achievement levels through setting higher goals.

4: Teachers think systematically about their practice and learn from experience.

When teachers reflect about their own teaching practices and then collaborate on planning schoolwide and systemwide approaches to assist learners in common sorts of need, they are contributing to massive professional development. This is the work of *professional* teachers—to shape the performance of the profession itself. Professional teachers are not represented by labor unions in professional decisions, but, rather, they represent themselves through their attention to detail and excellence. Professional teachers engage in ongoing inquiry about effective teaching. Professional teachers are never satisfied with just getting by but are only content when maximum excellence is achieved. Professional teachers want to be a part of a profession wherein all members hold themselves individually and collectively accountable for the best possible performance. Professional teachers are not about setting blame but are all about finding success. Professional teachers serve the students whatever it takes.

Professional teachers work with and within their communities to build successful schools. They want to assess their own growth in teaching skill and ability to seek even more effective approaches and methods. They undertake professional development plans without direction, just because they want to know more about their professional performance potential. They are the models of lifelong learning that we want our students to become.

Teaching professionals participate in true professional associations that inform them about best professional practices. Their concerns are not about labor representation but about maximum student learning. If they must, they tolerate imposed unions and may, perhaps, seek to turn them away from labor confrontation into a tool for true professional development. But even when labor groups put restrictions on professional performance, professional teachers perform anyway because they are accountable to a higher source— themselves as teaching professionals.

5: Teachers are members of learning communities.

One of the biggest challenges for classroom teachers is that of isolation. However one might seek to organize and operate the local school, when the teaching begins, teachers close the classroom door and begin to focus on the 15 to 50 precious lives placed into their hands for the designated learning period. Promoting real professionalism and collegiality among K–12 teachers was always one of the most challenging of activities for me as a K–12 instructional leader. The teaching act requires that teachers be minutely focused on the content and processes of teaching. But the larger picture of learning outcomes for the local community of students, the larger school, the state, and the nation is also important because the collective output of all the teachers of all our U.S. schools has the effect of determining the future of our nation. The work of education resides in wider communities. Educational societies, subject-based national organizations, political entities, and professional groups all have a stake in what our schools produce. Therefore, effective teachers seek ways to be plugged in to groups like the National Council for Social Studies Education, the National Science Foundation, the National Council for Teachers of English, and the National Mathematics Council, as well as university-related organizations helping to inform educational change and reform through research and publications. Effective teachers resist the temptation to close their doors at 4 p.m. and go home to plop themselves in front of the TV for 6 or 7 hours. They read, they think, they reflect, and they are involved in larger communities of educational interest. If they have already attained advanced degrees, then perhaps they serve to mentor others into the profession.

When teachers collaborate with other professionals about education, then they enhance their own performance and the profession as well. Teachers ought to have key roles in the very development of the curriculum frameworks and guides that are handed out by the state educational agencies' policy divisions. Truly *professional* teachers share responsibility with state educational authorities and educational leaders in shaping the content and the process standards that are the very foundation of all state public schools. If teachers have not been key players in developing standards, the National Board feels there may be legitimate question about their appropriateness for inclusion in our schools. But the teachers must be willing to acquire the necessary expertise, reflect and grow from their own practices, and then put themselves forward to become involved in such decision-making bodies at school-district level, county level, state level, and, perhaps, even national levels.

But excellent teachers also know how and when to draw personal lines, keep balance in their lives, and avoid becoming overextended. By working through groups and in larger communities, then, teachers lend their voices to larger constituencies that can share the broad development responsibilities.

A key role for teacher involvement is the ability to work collaboratively with parents in the preparation of children for learning excellence. Teachers need allies in the classroom, and the best allies are the parents. Effective teachers create strategies for engaging parents in decisions about their children's educational processes and progress. Frequent communication is the key to this collaboration. When teachers make sure that parents know all that is going on in classrooms and all that is expected of their children, then they build allegiance among parents to the learning the teacher is championing with their children.

The National Board for Professional Teaching promotes these five propositions and uses them in the designation of teachers who may become National Board-certified teachers. Information about these propositions and other NBPT activities can be found on their Web site, http://www.nbpts.org. A recent study by Dan Goldhaber and Emily Anthony (March 8, 2004) demonstrates that, in fact, the assessments of teaching and of teachers by the NBPT are on target. The study revealed that students taught by National Board-certified teachers made greater academic gains than their counterparts in other classrooms that had similar settings and demographics. Although one could challenge some of the conclusions from this investigation—for example, about whether the certification process makes the great teacher, or the great teacher is revealed by the certification process—one conclusion is assured. The standards of learning excellence, as measured by the NBPT core principles, are valid for identifying the necessary skills desired in all teachers. We will draw on these propositions and apply them throughout this book as we discuss the various models, methods, and strategies that creative, effective teachers may collect and use to *hit the target* of excellence in student learning outcomes.

CULTURAL AND LINGUISTIC DIVERSITY AND TEACHING EFFECTIVENESS

The NBPT propositions, as well as most state standards for public school teaching, require a philosophical orientation that is student centered, as opposed to subject centered. This is not to say subject content is unimportant; rather, *each and every* individual learner in a class must be taught the subject content so that learning potential outcomes are maximized. All learners deserve to have high-level outcomes arise from their schooling experiences, regardless of how they come to the school. Many communities have many children in schools whose first language is not English. Each deserves maximized learning outcomes. In addition, many communities have schools serving large numbers of children who have been historically disenfranchised because of economic limitations. Some theorists (Lindsey, Robins, & Terrell, 2003) suggest that these limitations come as part of a racism package in North American society. Others (Elliott & Holtrop, 1999) suggest that these limitations result from a general devolution in human nature in which people lack an appropriate orientation toward the creator's supremacy. Whatever the perceived cause, the truth is that many children are not well served in our schools, and it is our dream and vision to change so that *all* are served well.

Randall Lindsey and his colleagues (Lindsey et al., 2003) have suggested four very important tools that professional educators should make use of to achieve an appropriate attitude toward *cultural proficiency*. To these theorists, cultural proficiency is a view of living daily in ways that help us understand and appropriately respond to people who are different from us. For teachers, this is an essential skill. Of course, cultural proficiency addresses ethnic differences, linguistic differences, and social class differences, but it also could be applied to learning style differences. It is precisely such a skill that, when correctly applied, empowers teachers to individualize teaching for each learner, according to several learning-style sets and their several cultural divergences.

Lindsey et al. (2003) call these four tools *continuum, essential elements, guiding principles*, and *barriers*. Continuum involves a cultural-proficiency scale that illustrates ways in which people might address differences:

- Cultural destructiveness: See the difference, stomp it out
- Cultural incapacity: See the difference, make it wrong
- Cultural blindness: See the difference, act like you don't
- Cultural pre-competence: See the difference, respond inadequately
- Cultural competence: See the difference, understand the difference that difference makes
- Cultural proficiency: See the differences and respond positively and affirmatively. (p. 7)

For Lindsey and his colleagues (2003) in the Cultural Proficiency Group (culturalproficiency@earthlink.net), *cultural* proficiency can never be attained by following a formula or reorganizing a school according to a specific model. In the beginning of their excellent book *Cultural Proficiency: A Manual for School Leaders,* they proclaim plainly:

Cultural proficiency is not a plug-and-play model. Schools that adapt the cultural proficiency model for responding to the issues of diversity make a commitment to change the culture of the school. The individual and the organization must grow and change to be culturally proficient. (p. xxii)

The teacher who will become *culturally proficient* and teach accordingly is the teacher who will adopt a child-centered philosophy for teaching and become willing and equipped to *do whatever it takes* to reach each learner. Different religious and philosophical paradigms will suggest differing means by which such a state of being can be achieved, but the reality is that teachers must truly make positive differences in the lives of each and every child. Regardless of philosophical position, to become this *culturally proficient* teacher, you've got to desire it and be willing to undergo personal change to accomplish it. At its base, teaching is a life of selflessness and servant-heartedness. The culturally proficient teacher must be the teaching servant. Arrogance and self-centeredness, self-righteousness, and perceptions of self as above anyone else must be eliminated.

MULTIPLE MODELS TO CREATE A MYRIAD OF METHODS AND STRATEGIES

The national teaching standards and all state standards call on teachers to become effective at teaching and motivating student learning outcomes. All sets of standards specify that teachers must be knowledgeable about teaching methodologies—collections of methods and strategies they can use to prepare learning activities that best fit the diverse needs of diverse students from diverse communities and cultures.

This collection of teaching models provides several very well-recognized models or patterns for lesson design. These patterns are not prescriptions but rather examples for use by knowledgeable teachers who know the needs of their students. The first issue we must master if we are to become effective teachers is the development of safe, orderly, and well-managed learning environments. That will be discussed in Chapter 2. The next area we must cover deals with learning objectives or outcomes and the design of learning activities. That will be presented in Chapter 3. Following that, we will begin an introduction of several key models for lesson design that emerging effective teachers can use to prepare lessons aimed at specific learners, with specific needs, and specific curricula.

Classroom Management Strategies and Student Behavior

Guiding Questions

1. How do effective teaching techniques relate to classroom environment and management?

2. What are some useful and effective student behavior management techniques?

3. How might classroom standards or expectations for success differ from the older concept of classroom rules?

4. What do the National Board for Professional Teaching propositions suggest for classroom management and effective student learning?

5. How would you describe a golden rule classroom?

6. What is the relationship among classroom arrangement, organization for instruction, the facilitation of effective student conduct, and effective learning outcomes?

Proposition 2 of the National Board for Professional Teaching calls on effective teachers—people who know what to teach and how to deliver it—to maintain an effective learning environment. One of the key actions that contributes to accomplishing this is *establishing and maintaining standards for student behavior.* Effective teachers pay attention to students and strive to understand the reasons for student behavior. The standards of behavior always reflect the learning needs of the class. Teachers are consistent and fair with enforcement and intervene when student behavior does not meet agreed-upon classroom standards. Students are involved in making decisions about classroom procedures. With their management strategies, these effective teachers help all students learn to solve problems and resolve conflicts. They help students to exercise personal responsibility. They are careful to include families in the development, monitoring, and enforcement of personal responsibility for students.

It is often said among teachers that the first and foremost component of excellent classroom discipline is the *well-planned lesson.* The rest of these chapters will focus on well-planned lessons following a variety of models. However, even the best of teachers must at some time face an inattentive, distracted, disturbed, or unruly student. After many years of assisting new teachers to achieve professional competence, one point in particular has become clear to me. Without personal confidence in his or her ability to manage classroom activities for 20 or 30 energetic children or teenagers, no one can teach successfully. This chapter is placed at the beginning of our quiver of targeted teaching tools so that you can understand and see yourself as a successful classroom manager. Then, you can plan your well-made, accurately focused, and targeted lessons with confidence.

Discipline has always been a significant challenge facing teachers. For the past 20 years, discipline has ranked among the top two or three items of concern in annual polls about the quality of public schooling across the nation. In earlier decades, teachers were sent out with limited background in pedagogy and even less training in procedures for creating and maintaining attention to learning in the classroom. Over the past three decades, however, millions of teachers in America have developed, shared, or been taught effective discipline and classroom management processes. Many report reducing classroom misconduct by 80%.

The root of this approach to classroom management has been largely characterized as behaviorist because it tends to follow the notions presented in the behavioral psychology of B. F. Skinner. The implementation of certain types of rewards or consequences for various actions that are or are not desired is certainly part of that psychological domain. It is wise, therefore, for teachers always to remember that students are human beings with reason, will, and the ability to make moral choices, rather than animals acting on impulses for self-preservation. Classroom strategies should be carefully couched in a psychological approach that recognizes and expresses respect for individuals. Care should be taken that consequences are not demeaning or mean-spirited and that they are, indeed, appropriate and legal. Standards for effective teaching are based on the philosophical orientation of respect for students. Effective teachers manage classrooms effectively *because* they *respect* their students.

A SIMPLE PLAN FOR
CLASSROOM MANAGEMENT

A classroom management plan includes:

- Rules or standards
- Consequences
- Rewards
- Seating and room arrangements
- Classroom procedures

The classroom management plan should be put into writing and worked out in collaboration with the instructional leader of the school. Of utmost importance is to *explain the rationale.* The plan may be written in a style appropriate for distribution to parents and students—or in the form of notes to guide a teacher in presenting, explaining, and reinforcing its elements. However, a good idea is to send the classroom management plan home with students on the first day of school. To communicate most effectively, the plan should be accompanied with a cover letter addressed to parents that offers helpful suggestions that would help them support student learning and invites parents to be teammates in teaching students.

MANAGEMENT OF STUDENT CONDUCT

Effective teachers respond in ways that meet their own immediate needs in managing the classroom, yet do not violate the best interests of students. Teachers clearly and firmly communicate wants and needs to students and are prepared to back their words with action. They "say what they mean and mean what they say."

Effective teachers believe that all children have a right to learn. Therefore, these teachers are committed to the following precepts:

- No child should inhibit another child from learning for any reason.
- No child should engage in behavior that is not in his or her best interest or the best interests of others for any reason.
- Teachers should do what works!

Ineffective teachers, by contrast, fail to communicate their wants and needs clearly and firmly—or are not prepared to back their words with action. They respond to student challenges or thoughtlessness in a manner that meets their own immediate needs but that violates students' best interests.

With most discipline problems, words alone simply will not work. A teacher needs an overall discipline plan that covers expected behaviors, allows for possible rewards, and sets consequences, that is, what he or she will do if a student behaves inappropriately. Ineffective teachers merely threaten repeatedly, or, at the other extreme, overreact and kick the student out of class. Effective teachers, using a plan, inform a student that unacceptable conduct has been noted and an appropriate response will be forthcoming. Effective teachers center their attention on students who conduct themselves appropriately.

Management of students in a large group setting is a challenge, to be sure. Effective teachers do this well because of detailed planning for the process and because of a deep, abiding respect for the pupils. Some questions are asked consistently by teachers yearning for an effective classroom management process, and these are the common practices that have evolved in response.

- *What if a student will not look at the teacher when the teacher delivers an assertive message?* It does not matter; the teacher still delivers the message. The key to delivering the message is the fact that the teacher looks at the student, not vice versa.

- *What if the parents will not support stronger discipline?* Teachers have the right to parent support and must insist on it. Teachers must let a parent know that they cannot tolerate disruptive behavior from the child of any parent. Teachers need to communicate their belief that the parent agrees with this concept.

- *How do teachers get the support of their principal?* Teachers have a right to the support of their principal. They should share their discipline plan with the principal and get approval before putting the plan into action. They must also determine what the administrator will do when students are sent to the office. Teachers and administrators should collaborate, together with other members of the school team, on a schoolwide discipline plan.

- *How can a teacher justify sending a student to the principal for only touching or talking?* If a student's behavior, even if it is only talking, stops you from teaching, it is a serious disruption. All it takes is two or three students continuously touching, talking, or the like to stop teaching and learning from taking place. (Special note: All referrals to the principal must be accompanied by the understanding that the teacher will call and speak to the parent at the first available opportunity. Also, except in case of severe disruption, referral to the principal should follow other elements, as described later in this chapter.) Having a clear disciplinary plan and understanding of what warrants a visit to the principal's office is the best preventative measure.

- *What does a teacher do if many students disrupt at once?* Simply put all their names on the board and let the students know you mean business. It is important to emphasize that when a teacher becomes more assertive, students quickly stop their disruptions.

- *What if a student earns four checks (calling for a visit to the administrator's office) and will not leave the room?* Teachers must have a plan for removing students from the room when they are disruptive. Especially on the secondary level, teachers must meet with the administrator and determine a specific plan of action to remove a belligerent student from a classroom. Without a plan, many teachers are at the mercy of hostile students.

- *What if a teacher does not want to stay after school with disruptive students?* That teacher should not face the need to stay after school as a consequence in the plan. The teacher must be comfortable with the plan and each of its components.

- *What if a student is supposed to stay after school and does not stay?* Typically, effective teachers would have the students stay twice as long the next day or send the student to the principal.

- *What if the student curses at the teacher? Does the teacher just put the student's name on the board?* All discipline plans should include a "severe clause." This clause states that a student who severely disrupts class goes immediately to the principal.

- *Do you openly praise secondary students who behave?* Most secondary students do not like to be praised openly. The teacher must reinforce the behavior more subtly.

Across the past two decades, growing misuse of the practices outlined above has led to criticisms of their behaviorist roots. The strategies and techniques are good, but we make a serious error when we begin to treat human beings in a mechanistic way or as the objects of experimental stimuli. Skinner's work with animals does not necessarily transfer to people. Also, there is the dimension of human emotion and rationality. Humans can determine to do things *in spite* of stimuli they know they are about to receive, rather than because of it.

Recognizing the stages of development and ability is also necessary, as recommended by cognitive investigators such as Piaget. Some students may not respond to certain stimuli because they lack ability or developed skills. For example, teachers often speak harshly to a misbehaving teenager and then ask, "Why did you do that?" The typical teenage answer is "I don't know." The fact is, he or she is telling the truth. Teens are not prepared to understand their actions and explain the things that cause them to act or misbehave. They simply respond according to their personal development and experiences. The teacher influences behavior by teaching students how to consider and understand their actions.

EXPECTATIONS FOR SUCCESSFUL CLASSROOMS

Effective teachers have simple, clear statements of academic and conduct expectations for the members of their classroom communities. They are few in number and broadly and positively stated. The rules of a class often reflect the inner philosophical orientation of the teacher regarding the place of learners in our society. Some teachers impose a long list of explicit things to be done or avoided. Conduct in such classrooms tends to be highly regulated, but the rules are often challenged. More successful teachers have just a few broadly stated propositions that cover most situations and that are reviewed frequently with the students. These teachers may not even call such statements *rules*, but refer to them as *expectations* or *standards* instead. Depending on the maturity and ability of the class members, effective teachers often involve students in extensive discussion regarding the expectations and their importance. Rules, expectations, or standards should establish a tone for classroom function. They should give all students a sense of a protected environment wherein each learner's opportunities are valued and guarded.

Effective teachers successfully use general classroom expectations or responsibilities. Such teachers develop in students a conscious awareness of acceptable classroom behaviors as a necessary precursor to their own successful learning. The expectation or standard is looked on as a foundation that can be expanded and related to any and all circumstances. For example, a teacher posting a long list of *don'ts* might say, "Don't talk unless given permission to do so by the teacher." This is fine until the teacher forgets to tell students that it is acceptable during a work period to discuss work with neighbors—something students do naturally, without being told to do so. Students then learn, perhaps unconsciously, that there is a stated rule, and there are unwritten exceptions—but they are unsure of themselves because the teacher has failed to clarify. Better is a teacher who says, "Students will work and communicate *appropriately* in given situations." With that class standard in place, a teacher frequently uses the foundational concept to reinforce and train appropriate and inappropriate responses.

We should limit classroom standards or rules to a number that the teacher and students can readily remember without prompting. Many say that there should never be more than five, whereas others opt for three or fewer. If more than five standards seem to be needed, the teacher might reconsider wording. Perhaps some statements of the standards can be clustered into more broadly worded concepts that are easy to remember and readily applied to varying circumstances.

A new teacher named Charles came into teaching later than his colleagues. He had been in two other brief careers: the ministry and the military. As he began teaching in the lower elementary grades, he discovered that these young children were able to respond to big ideas like *respect* and *appreciation* and *safety*. During his first year, he had the typical struggles to discover an effective pattern of class management. In part, because he had third-, fourth-, fifth-, and sixth-grade students in the same room, students had differing abilities to respond to his directions and understand his intentions. After about 6 months, Charles called a class community meeting. He asked the students to list the problems they had been having that were causing the teacher to have to waste class time with warnings and punishments.

The students accurately listed all of the offenses. The teacher then asked the students to describe how they wanted the teacher to act toward them. Next, he asked them to explain how they wanted each of the other students to act toward them. Finally, he grouped them by their age groups and had them develop a common list of the common elements. From that activity, done in desperation, came the Team E Standards of Class Conduct. The students recognized what they wanted done to them, and Charles easily connected that to how they should act toward others. The fact that Charles was willing to have groups of students list standards for his own conduct toward them created a special bond. Classroom instruction went much more smoothly the rest of the year. Because third-grade students stayed with Charles across their remaining

3 years in elementary school, by the time they reached sixth grade, the class was highly self-managing. All of this came out of two classroom standards: (a) respect others as I wish to be respected, and (b) do what I came here to do.

SETTING LIMITS AS A KEY TO SUCCESS

Part of the communications process in a good discipline plan involves establishing limits. The process begins on the very first day of class. Effective teachers systematically and consistently develop and establish limits so that all can function comfortably. Following are guidelines for effective limit setting, consequences, and reminders.

Guidelines for Setting Effective Limits

- The teacher must feel comfortable with all elements in the limits and consequences.
- Negative consequences should be something the child does not like, but not something physically or psychologically harmful.
- Negative consequences and positive reinforcements should be provided to the child as a choice.
- Consequences must follow immediately after the child chooses to disregard the teacher's request or direction.
- Consequences must be provided in a matter-of-fact manner without hostility, screaming, and so on.
- Consequences can be used a maximum of three times.
- Consequences are always part of a limit-setting hierarchy.
- The hierarchy should include a maximum of five levels of reminders and consequences.
- The limit-setting hierarchy must contain a "severe clause" in case of a severe disruption; the clause leads to immediate referral to the principal.
- Referral to the principal is always the last consequence, after all other reminders are exhausted.
- The principal must always approve the teacher's discipline and limit-setting plan in advance.
- The discipline plan is always communicated to students and presented in writing to parents prior to implementation.
- If there is general lack of cooperation and attentiveness among students after 3 days and the plan does not bring general change, the teacher should make it stricter and share changes with the principal, students, and parents.

In the plan shown in Figure 2.1, one successful classroom veteran, Dan, created a suggested hierarchy of increasing consequences and initiated it with a bit of facetious humor. He began with something that all teachers have; some

Figure 2.1   Sample Reminder Plan

Introduction

"In our class this year, we will live within our adopted three rules. Sometimes students forget themselves and need reminders. I use the following system of reminders. (Point to the boxed plan, below, which is posted in the front of the room.)

"It begins with 'the stare.'" (Show emotionless, expressionless face with eyes focused directly on one student. Refocus this look on many students in turn, always holding until two-way eye contact is achieved and the student looks away.)

"This does not mean I am angry; I am simply insisting that you return to being a responsible learner. If you do, the matter will be immediately forgotten."

Reminders	
0	"The Stare" (informal warning)
1	name on the board (formal warning)
2	one check—15 minutes after school or at recess
3	two checks—30 minutes after school
4	three checks—the above plus a call to parents
5	four checks—removal to principal

Again, be sure to have a clear understanding with your principal about what warrants a student's visit to the principal's office.

call it a "teacher look" or a "mean look" or an "oh-oh look" or something similar. Because most parents also have such a look, it can be effective when used by a teacher, initially introduced with humor. Students usually giggle and laugh at this exaggerated demonstration of "the stare," but the message is communicated. It is not uncommon later in a term for the teacher to be administering "the stare" and for one student to gently jibe the culprit by whispering, "Hey, you're getting 'the stare'!" The behavior ceases. Note that in this sample plan, the possibility of removal to the principal would have been prearranged.

RESPONDING TO BEHAVIORAL CHALLENGES

Responses to behavioral challenges fall into nine categories. These categories are planned ignoring, signal interference, proximity control, interest boosting, direct appeal to personal or family values, support through humor, support by routines, removal of seductive objects, supportive removal, and disciplinary removal with parent conference.

Planned Ignoring

Ignoring, coupled with regular practice of positive reinforcement, calls on the teacher to judge which behaviors are tolerable and which must be addressed. The teacher looks for positive instances and then reinforces students who are found to be functioning positively. Minor occurrences are usually ignored, although the definition of *minor* may vary from teacher to teacher. It all relates to the basic concept that the teacher must be comfortable in the class, and the teacher must ensure that students are comfortable in the class. Behaviors that threaten the comfort level or that distract learners are not tolerated.

Signal Interference

Signal interference involves a look or a gesture, a facial expression or prolonged eye contact, facing the body squarely toward the offending student. It is effective when there is a well-established and understood code of conduct and system of penalties as well as rewards.

Proximity Control

In proximity control, the teacher, without stopping his or her act of teaching, moves closer and closer to the student until the behavior stops. Stopping the behavior is the goal, not punishing learners or embarrassing them. Proximity of the teacher might be adjusted several times until the teacher is virtually teaching within arm's reach of the offending student.

Interest Boosting

Interest boosting involves a positive approach by the teacher with the intent of more directly engaging the learner in the task at hand. It might be done with a series of questions or a suggestion that certain things be done.

Direct Appeal to Values

The teacher may refer the misbehaving student directly to a common set of acceptable values and behaviors. Next, the teacher leads the student to assess whether or not he or she is adhering to those values. This requires that the student have a capability for values orientation. Learners whose background and experiences consist of negative orientations in valuing may have difficulty recognizing the rightness of anything except that which meets the individual's momentary personal wants.

Support Through Humor

Teachers who see humor in otherwise stressful or conflict situations will be able to provide support to students through humor. Care must be taken, however, that the humor is not at the expense of any student or other individual.

Support by Routines

Effective teachers create clear and regular operational procedures that students can count on. Once this has been done, support by routines is an important management strategy. If learners understand how they are to function and can see the benefits in doing so, they usually follow sensible routines.

Removal of Seductive Objects

Taking away a distracting object is a time-honored way for teachers to maintain attention on learning on the part of both the distracted student and classmates.

Supportive Removal

Sometimes called "time out," supportive removal means that the teacher takes the student out of the problem situation. Like the previous three responses, this approach emphasizes problem solution, not punishment.

Disciplinary Removal and Parent Conference

Contact with parents is usually a useful and productive activity. This element need not be held until last. Parents desire early input into management of their child's conduct. A time may also come when it is necessary to suspend a child from class and initiate extensive behavioral counseling.

CONSEQUENCES FOR SEVERE PROBLEMS

Not often but occasionally, teachers must take stronger positions with confused and misdirected students to bring about the necessary climate for learning so that *all* children learn well in the classroom. Some additional ideas for consequences that serve as more intense reminders of required responsible conduct include in-school suspension, recording behavior, sending to another classroom, behavior contracting, and parent presence in the classroom.

In-School Suspension

Some schools have a room monitored by an administrator and/or teachers where students do academic work in silence. Disruption in the isolation room brings three more hours in isolation. The student does not participate in recess or lunch, eats alone, and is escorted to the restroom.

Recording Behavior

A video or audio recorder is placed next to the student and turned on if he or she becomes disruptive. The tape of the disruption is later played for parents and the principal.

Sending to Another Classroom

The disruptive student is sent, by prearrangement, to do work isolated in another classroom. This other classroom is an alternative to the principal's office, and the strategy is planned with that classroom's teacher. The student is sent with academic work to a well-run classroom at a widely different grade level for approximately 30 minutes. The student sits alone at the back of class, facing the wall, and does the assigned work.

Behavior Contracting and Parent Presence in the Class

Behavior contracting is an option that may be introduced in a behavioral conference with the family. After all are in agreement and understand what the offenses are and that change is necessary, the teacher, student, and parents can begin to develop a listing of what should be stopped, what should be done, and what will happen in either case. Many who lean toward a behaviorist approach would consider using positive reinforcements and rewards as the student is able to demonstrate systematic reduction in offending incidents. The principle of *extinction* is part of an overall *behavior modification* concept. But behaviors can return after having been supposedly extinct; therefore, it is necessary to help the student recognize causes of unacceptable behaviors.

A behavior contract can provide *recognition* strategies that the student should follow when behavior is questioned. Contracts are aimed at helping out-of-control students to discover ways of managing themselves and remaining within acceptable boundaries of conduct.

Many teachers have found it necessary, and quite productive, to ask a parent to sit in class on repeated occasions to notice the child's behavior patterns. Such observation times are then followed by intensive planning between the teacher and the parent, as well as other professional resource people, to create success for the child.

POSITIVE REINFORCEMENTS

For effective classroom management, teachers praise and give attention to students who are complying with expectations but do not consistently praise the *same* cooperative student—it is wiser to spread the praise around. Older students are best praised confidentially and subtly, in private. Praise must be backed up with positive follow-through. One Southern California teacher made a career practice of sending home two "Good-Guy-Grammes" each day.

A Teacher's Experience: Good-Guy-Grammes

It started as an accidental discovery. Georgie had been having problems all year. One day, after Christmas vacation, Georgie returned to school and was particularly well behaved. He was so much improved that Dan developed a note to the parents, whom he had phoned many times regarding Georgie's misbehavior. He hastily wrote a note thanking Georgie and his parents for the change in attitude and class participation that was shown that day. As a second thought, Dan scripted *Good-Guy-Gramme* across the top of the note.

The next day, Georgie, his mother, and his father came to the office and asked the principal to see Georgie's teacher. The principal, not knowing what had transpired, presumed that the matter was over a question about how Dan must have disciplined Georgie (again). The parents wouldn't say much to him, only that they had to see the teacher as soon as possible. Dan was paged to the office at the next recess break.

Much to the principal's surprise, Georgie's father walked up to Dan, shook his hand, and tearfully thanked him for having such a positive impact on Georgie. Then, his mother did the same and handed Dan a cake that she and Georgie had baked the night before. Dan was as much befuddled as was the principal. Finally, Dan thanked them for their words and asked what had happened.

They explained that there had been a death in the family the month prior to the Christmas break and that Georgie had taken the death quite hard. They had always responded to Dan's earlier calls and notes about problems but hadn't shared any of this personal information. Then, after Christmas, Georgie had seemed to notice that his teacher, although frequently disciplining him, always showed him respect and that "he never puts me down." When Dan had taken the time to notice in writing the improvement in Georgie's behavior, it had made a profound impression on the lad, and the parents as well.

From that day forward, Dan made a point of sending home *Good-Guy-Grammes* to all students whenever they showed positive behavior and especially when they showed improvement from problem behavior.

Marbles, chips, or buttons dropped into a jar whenever the class is doing well is a widespread practice. Many teachers give directions for assignments, then reinforce with marbles. This is most frequently done when teachers use cooperative learning and the class is grouped in regular study teams. Rewards are given by team for accumulated team performance. Teachers may use peer pressure: "If there are no names on the board, we will get five marbles." The counters are tallied at the end of each day, and a running total is maintained. When counters achieve a predesignated level, a reward is given to the entire class. Although the class may earn the first reward quickly, the next reward should come after achieving a higher goal. The teacher gradually increases the expectation to higher levels. Rewards, however, must be something students want.

Various packaged materials about classroom discipline are on the market, but all essentially use these components:

- Clear standards
- Clear and frequent communication
- Reinforcement of student responsibility
- Reminders
- Increasing consequences
- Rewards

In virtually all successful discipline plans, great teachers manage to spend more time positively reinforcing students than negatively reinforcing them. Although fear may be psychologically motivating in the short run, encouragement brings more lasting results.

Effective teachers have found other, less direct strategies useful in maintaining appropriate classroom decorum. Some individuals may find these less desirable, but they do have a proven track record. These strategies include classroom procedures, a teacher's standards of dress and mental attitude, and teaming with colleagues.

SCHOOL CODES OF CONDUCT

Most schools and districts have created codes of conduct or policies that guide the formation of classroom and school behavior standards for students. The code developed by the Charleston County School District can be found at their Web site (http://www.charleston.k12.sc.us/topic.cfm?topic_id=38&sub_topic_id=214#cofc).

PROFESSIONAL DEVELOPMENT AND CLASSROOM MANAGEMENT

Teaching standards speak not only to classroom performance but also to the overall professional attitudes of the professional teacher. Many teachers in classrooms across this nation fit this mold, but, unfortunately, just as many do not. The standards movement has been instrumental in bringing about a clearly articulated understanding of just what a true educational professional looks like. Effective teaching begins with attitudes and dispositions about learners and includes ideas that influence learners for positive learning outcomes. We commonly call this part of effective teaching *class management.* Many people know a great deal about a subject but cannot teach it because they cannot set up group learning activities with planned strategies to influence and manage the learning environment.

Effective teachers carefully reflect on their teaching practices. They actively and consistently engage in planning their own professional development. Teachers establish professional learning goals for themselves. They frequently pursue opportunities to develop professional knowledge and skill. Effective teachers learn about and work with local communities to improve their professional practice. Effective teachers communicate effectively with families and involve them in student learning and the school community. Effective teachers contribute to school activities, promote school goals, and improve professional practice by working collegially with all school staff. Also, effective teachers balance professional responsibilities and maintain motivation and commitment to all students. Let's revisit the fourth and fifth NBPT propositions within the framework of professional development.

4: Teachers think systematically about their practice and learn from experience.

When effective teachers reflect on their practices, they assess their own professional growth as teachers. They try to learn about teaching through observing and interacting with their students, as well as through observing colleagues. They ponder their instructional successes and dilemmas to move their professional practices forward. Careful analyses are made to understand what contributes to student learning. Effective teachers will formulate professional development plans that are based on all this thoughtful reflection.

When teachers are effective in their practices, it is because they maintain an attitude of lifelong learning. They seek to learn more about professional roles and responsibilities. As they establish goals, they seek out opportunities for professional growth and development. They make use of professional literature and other professional development opportunities to increase understanding of teaching and learning. Their purpose is to continue seeking out and refining approaches that make the curriculum accessible to every student.

5: Teachers are members of learning communities.

Effective teachers work within communities to improve professional practice. One can see in the effective teacher's class activities evidence that he or she values and respects the student's community and appreciates its role in student learning. Effective teachers will work to gain more understanding of the cultures and dynamics of their students' communities. They find creative ways to promote collaboration between school and community. When opportunities or needs arise, they will identify and use school, district, and local community social service resources to benefit students and their family. Many creative teachers have been successful in seeking out resources from the local community and businesses to support their students' learning. A powerful key in effective teaching is that teachers frequently interact with students in activities outside the classroom.

A Teacher's Experience: Rosita and the "Smart Things of the World"

Donna was a seventh-grade teacher at a Southern California urban school. She was noted for her long days, spending countless hours after school helping students who were struggling with their studies. She also had close contacts with local service clubs, where she often presented needs of particular students' families for eye care, health care, and other such services.

One of her students, a girl named Rosita, came from very poor family circumstances. Rosita had said on many occasions how much she wanted to get to know all the "smart things of the world" so she could also be a teacher like Donna. Donna would give Rosita a hug and then scurry her back to her learning tasks.

> One day, Rosita came in wearing a softball uniform. It seems that she had been given a chance to be on a girls' bobby sox team, and she so wanted to do that. However, she didn't know how to play very well. Donna contacted some of her friends in the softball league and found out where there was going to be a clinic. She made arrangements with Rosita's family to take her to the softball clinic on the following weekend.
>
> Donna described with glee the day she sat in the stands on a weekend and watched her student, Rosita, play first base in a league championship game. What did that have to do with classroom learning? If you asked Donna, she would tell you "everything."

6: Teachers work with families to improve professional practice.

For as long as there have been teachers, effective ones have demonstrated in a myriad of ways how they value and respect their students and their students' families. Such teachers work to engage the family in learning activities because they recognize that families are the child's first and most lasting teachers. Teachers become aware of the things they need to know to better communicate with students' families.

Susan taught a third- and fourth-grade multiage class in a rural Southern California school district. One day, a new family came with a brother and sister who were in the two grades that Susan taught. Because of the small size of the school, this was the only class for both ages. The biggest problem was that the family spoke only Spanish, and the children spoke only the most rudimentary of English phrases. Susan's class included a fourth-grade girl who spoke fluent English although she was a native Spanish speaker. Of course, Susan asked her if she would be willing to assist the two new children. As the year went on, I noticed Susan rushing out of school much earlier than usual every Tuesday and Thursday. After a couple of weeks, I found occasion to ask her why she was leaving so much earlier than everyone else. What a joy it was to listen to her explain her progress in a conversational Spanish course at the local high school, which she was taking so she could better communicate with her new students and their families.

Servant leaders come at all levels of an organization, and Susan was being a servant leader by extending herself to gain language skills needed to help her pupils. That is certainly professional practice at its highest level.

7: Effective teachers work with colleagues to improve professional practice.

Collegiality has not been tolerated among public school teachers until very recently. Teacher unions have been so aggressive in opposing administrators that any attempts by teachers to serve as coaches and evaluators of other teachers have been met with huge political pressures against the districts and contract language that prevented such relationships among teachers. New laws in many states, prompted by teaching standards, are changing all that, and now, peer coaching, peer assistance, and even peer evaluation are being undertaken with rapidly increasing frequency. The truth is, however, that *effective* teachers have *always* created opportunities to collaborate with colleagues about teaching. Those colleagues included administrators, specialists, and even paraprofessionals. Such professional teachers see it as their responsibility to influence the total product of the school, not just the 20 or 30 students in their class. They can frequently be found engaged in thoughtful dialogue and reflection with colleagues to solve teaching-related problems, theirs or the other teachers. They are equipped and prepared to participate in making and implementing schoolwide decisions or to contribute to schoolwide events and learning activities.

8: Effective teachers balance professional responsibilities and maintain personal motivation.

A potential weakness of the standards for teaching is that they are so all-encompassing that they produce a composite picture of a "super-teacher" that no single individual can replicate. All the standards reviewed in connection with this book should be seen as a composite and not an individual prescription for universal success. Different teachers will have diverse ways of measuring up to the various standards, but their end will be success for the students. An important element, therefore, is that effective teachers learn how to create balance in their personal and professional lives. They will take steps to reduce stress and maintain a positive attitude with students and colleagues by exercising choices. They will preserve time for their own families and their own health, as well. They will challenge themselves throughout their careers but will find ways to develop personally beyond the requisite professional skills.

Their personal conduct will be driven by high moral standards because they are aware of their impact as an example to their many students. They seek ways of modeling personal and professional integrity at every turn. They observe not only the laws but also the higher spirit of the best practices. They do this to maintain classrooms that are safe and inspiring to their learners.

Procedures for Success

There is much more to a safe and orderly classroom than prescriptions for a teacher to follow as he or she interacts with students about their behavior. Elements in a discipline plan differ from the components of each teacher's classroom management plan called procedures. A procedure, or routine, is the recommended, optimum process for accomplishing some rudimentary task. NBPT Proposition 2, in explaining how to maintain an effective learning environment, presents a key idea that effective teachers must undertake consistently: *planning and implementing classroom procedures and routines that support student learning.* Daily schedules, time lines, classroom routines, and classroom rules are created in ways that involve all the students. Teachers then help students to internalize classroom rules, routines, and procedures so they can become self-directed learners. A climate of fairness and respect is generated by classroom procedures and the effective teacher's consistent attitude. Procedures are held as flexible standards and not rigid rules in order to help each student uniquely, equitably, but in fairness to all others.

Students are usually neither penalized nor rewarded for following or not following a procedure. Procedures tell students what to do when they need to use the restroom, finish work early, break a pencil, hear the fire drill bell, turn in homework, or other such activities. Effective procedures help teachers create a smoothly running classroom. A smoothly running environment, in turn, helps students feel confident and secure in the room.

Procedures make up a large part of what Elliot Eisner (1985) calls *implicit curriculum*—information that is taught and learned but is not explicitly outlined in curriculum documentation. Procedures are also a large part of real life. Adults follow some of the same procedures that we establish for students, such as procedures for clear and courteous communication; orderly entry and exit of a room; completing complex tasks; being accountable; passing out paper or other supplies; returning from an absence; recording grades; correcting papers; moving around the classroom; or using a pencil sharpener, drinking fountain, or library. Effective classroom managers establish clear and precise procedures, thoughtfully developed to enable students' maximum achievement. Procedures need to be taught and learned so that achievement is maximized.

Effective teachers use three elements in teaching procedures:

- *Explaining procedures* calls on the teacher to state the procedure, demonstrate it, and check student understanding of it, as well as of each term used in presenting it.
- *Rehearsing* calls on teachers to repeatedly practice the procedure with students and to periodically review it.
- *Reinforcing* requires systematic recognition of students who are *doing it correctly* and a means for positively reminding learners who have not yet mastered the procedure; anything that a teacher wants students to routinely accomplish requires a procedure.

LOOK THE PART

At the risk of being accused that I am out of date, I wish to make some observations about teacher appearance and student conduct. It should be no surprise to us in our present-day, business-oriented culture to realize that appearance is an element in success. Yes, there are outstanding teachers who *could* teach successfully in blue jeans and a T-shirt, but they are the exception rather than the rule. Teachers should dress in a practical way yet an exemplary way for the professional modeling they are daily accomplishing with impressionable youth. In my humble opinion, teachers need to dress the part. Teachers who want learners and parents to treat them like professionals may want to actually *look like* professionals as well as engage in professional behavior. An individual has only one chance at a *first impression*, so one must look like a confident, aware professional from the very first meeting with the class.

How much credibility would a salesperson have if he approached customers wearing a T-shirt emblazoned with the phrase, "Stick it in your ear"? We are client-servers, and we must present an image in which our clients can have confidence. Lawyers, doctors, and all others we consider professionals dress up to the confidence level when presenting themselves professionally. Would a lawyer go into court wearing his comfortable, tattered sweatshirt and his prized 49-ers jacket? I think not. Should not teachers look like the molders of dreams and futures that they truly are? We *are* role models for our students in all things, even in dress.

One teacher entered into this discussion with me, emphasizing that he wore jeans and T-shirts so that students could "identify with him." I asked him what image he believed they held of him, given his informality. He believed that they saw him as a buddy. I wondered whether students really need another helpless peer or buddy—or if they need a *role model* who appears professional as he or she performs professionally. To be sure, there are nicely dressed teachers who do not perform well, but veteran effective teachers tell us that it is easier when they are *not* dressed casually, as though they were about to work in the yard or take a hike across the hillside.

One veteran teacher reports noticing in his first year of teaching that student conduct was less cooperative on days he wore casual attire than on days he dressed up. He began to keep track of the number of disciplinary conflicts and found that on days he wore a dress shirt, tie, and (temperature permitting) a coat, student disciplinary incidents were reduced by 25%. On days that he wore jeans and a T-shirt, there were out-and-out shouting matches with some of the more vociferous students. He quickly concluded that students would respond to him more as a professional if he looked like one.

In the 21st century, social mores are changing regarding dress styles and appearance. Yes, there are *effective teachers* who dress in casual clothing on a regular basis, but these teachers have many years of practice on which to rely in reaching and teaching their students. It would be good for inexperienced teachers to present themselves in a professional manner when trying to change lives.

COLLABORATE IN A TEAM

One of the elements of teaching used to be isolation. Some teachers managed classes effectively, and others not as well. A key understanding for effective teaching and learning emerging in the 21st century is that teachers must not work in isolation or individual private practice. They are part of a team. Thus, class management is part of a schoolwide decision that involves all of the educators at the school.

The vast majority of school systems across the country have begun to institutionalize methods of new teacher induction that have been practiced informally for a long time. Many teachers would say that they learned much more about teaching in the first year of full-time practice than in the preparation years, and that they learned it from seasoned veterans who took the rookie under a wise wing. The wise beginning teacher locates a skillful veteran and spends time learning from him or her. Many systems have identified mentor teachers who are given the responsibility of coaching rookies. Where that is not the case, a beginner might ask the principal who is the very best teacher on the faculty and then ask that teacher's permission to observe and learn. The rookie can ask the veteran to observe and give feedback. If the system permits, a new teacher may seek to become a part of a teaching team—three to five teachers who plan together, coach each other, and often share the same students.

Frequent feedback from skilled veterans helps a new teacher improve rapidly. The saddest fact about teacher interaction has been that the vast majority of teachers become isolated or isolate themselves in their classrooms, fearing to become professionally linked with other teachers. Fear of being observed must be overcome if one is to profit from the vast wealth of experience available among teaching colleagues. The first-year teacher, while trying to work with a particularly needy pupil, may wish to ask more experienced teachers of lower grades to suggest discipline approaches and strategies they found effective with that student. In turn, the beginner may bring new perspectives and ideas—and soon becomes a veteran, equipped and empowered to help another new recruit.

THE GOLDEN RULE AND CLASSROOM MANAGEMENT

During many years in the school administrator's office, I repeatedly heard four themes from the hundreds of children and teens who had gotten into trouble with their teacher. When I asked for reasons or explanations, I heard the following: "He just won't listen to me!" "She hates me!" "I made one mistake and she never let me forget it!" "I just can't seem to please him!"

Often, of course, these pleas were simply excuses. Nevertheless, adults, when dealing with the young, sometimes forget the pain and angst that children and teens experience just in growing up. We believe in setting high expectations and holding youngsters to high standards, as we should. However, we may forget to show our pupils the way over the rough terrain. The young have not come this way before, so they may need guidance rather than criticism and pressure.

A useful guideline for classroom management is the time-honored Golden Rule. Although we may have heard the phrasing in words reminiscent of the King James New Testament, "Do unto others as you would have others do unto you," the Golden Rule has been around in one form or another for millennia. Confucius, who worshipped ancestors; Plato and Aristotle, who were polytheist/atheists; Rabbi Hillel, an ancient Hebrew teacher who questioned God's presence; and an ancient Hindu epic poem, the Mahabharata—these provide only a few of the variations on the Golden Rule theme, which occurs in some formulation in most major religious faith and ethical systems. This adage, perhaps better known than practiced, is nevertheless an excellent precept for all social activities, including those involved in teaching. It calls for patience, respect, forgiveness, and love. The statement by Jesus Christ, quoted from the Book of Matthew in the New Testament, is unique among the versions for it calls on the individual to initiate the desirable action toward others without first considering how the others treat that individual. By contrast, a famous ancient Jewish rabbi's version, in the second century B.C., was "*don't* do to others what you wouldn't want done to you." The servant-hearted teacher does to others as he or she would want done, regardless of how the other has acted previously.

Whenever students in teacher education programs ask me how to manage a classroom, I am drawn into remembrances of past teachers I have observed, coached, supervised, or just had to live with. Those who were effective had a certain special quality that others might not identify. Some would call it a servant heart.

During a lesson, a young man, John, was distracted, not listening attentively, or at least not understanding the teacher's words. At one point, he raised a hand and asked about the instruction. The teacher, stopping abruptly in the middle of an explanation, rolled her eyes in disgust at the interruption and sighed, "Didn't I just finish explaining that? Where were you *this time,* Johnny?" Embarrassed, the boy retreated into a shell—confused, lost, and resolved that he would never again publicly admit that he had any questions whatsoever. Worse yet is what other students in the class may have learned from Johnny's humiliation. Whether they thought so consciously or not, all but the most confident among them would now refrain from the personal risk of asking a question when they became lost, fearing public humiliation from the teacher. No, that is not how classrooms are best managed. Rather, a Golden Rule teacher— to repeat the phrase—practices patience, respect, forgiveness, and love.

Patience

School teachers who would practice the Golden Rule must find sources from which they can be continuously recharged with energy, wisdom, and especially patience. The youngsters in most classrooms come from circumstances that were not as common in recent history as they are today. Children and youth are reacting like young, recently planted trees in a hurricane. They are pushed and blown by every wind of controversy, leaned on by those who make a life habit of abusing others, assailed with the flying debris from storms of political and social unrest. Forces far beyond their control often uproot them. Their teachers—those who would truly make a difference in their lives—must build windbreaks for them. Their teachers must be strong while they are weak. Their teachers must be consistent while the kids are tumbling across the landscape in search of new roots to hold them fast.

Respect

Another positive trait in a good class management plan is that the teacher shows respect for students' personhood, giving them the dignity of full attention to their comments and responses. It is easy to become distracted by the demands of monitoring and adjusting the learning situation. When that happens, when we realize we have been thinking about our next response rather than listening to our learners, we must catch ourselves. The child deserves our full, undivided attention.

The NBPT Proposition 2 includes a key idea: *establishing a climate that promotes fairness and respect.* When we discussed this earlier in Chapter 1, several illustrations were presented describing how effective teachers apply this principle. This is certainly a goal that *all effective teachers never surrender*—the need for each to be respectful toward the other, including those who may be different from them. These teachers model and promote such respect and fairness. They demonstrate respect by carefully considering how they approach each individual student. They recognize effort and achievement by every member of the class and reinforce contributions that lead to meaningful learning. Effective teachers consistently recognize and respond to inappropriate conduct in ways that are fair and equitable.

Back to our young man, Johnny. The teacher could have asked him, smiling, to restate the purpose of the lesson. Next, she might have posed a series of questions to reconstruct the train of thought she had covered up to that point. She next could have patiently checked this learner's understanding by asking him to recite the issue, as he understood it. She could have reassured Johnny by thanking him for the question, assuming that others may have been confused. This approach to student questions, even for inattentive students, demonstrates concern and love for the individual learner. Such a response fits within a plan of positive discipline and behavior modification. Teachers are well advised to demonstrate this respectful attitude toward each and every student.

Forgiveness

Another practice of a Golden Rule teacher is forgiveness. This quality calls on teachers to move past situations in which learners have let them down. Such teachers never hold a grudge. In other words, I must not look down on a learner today because of his or her disappointing or inappropriate responses on previous days.

Today, teachers are often quite up-front about judgments of certain students and their families. Sitting in many teacher lunchrooms, one may hear conversation (gossip, really) in which even well-meaning teachers sometimes castigate their students.

But I am arguing that teachers must model forgiveness. Every day must be a new day for our learners. We must not write off any of these youngsters; we must allow no throw-aways in our schools.

Love

The word *love* is used in many ways to mean many things in Western cultures today. Here we have a very specific, high-aimed definition for this word in the use of schooling. Love for us means the selfless regard for others—the students or learners—over and above concern and regard for self-interests and personal desires. Teachers who love their students make the necessary commitments to ensure their success. This could be described as the proverbial Golden Rule teacher—one who teaches students using methods and relationships that the teacher would have liked to experience as a learner.

The Golden Rule teacher's commitment is: "I will love you—that is, regard you above my own personal interests—regardless of your situation, what you look like, how you act, or how you treat me." To discipline a child without love is not to discipline at all, but rather, to abuse. Without love—the selfless concern for the best interests of the other person—one will lack credibility and will be unable to effect a permanent, positive change in the behavior of another.

Patience, respect, forgiveness, and love are characteristics that set outstanding teachers apart from the crowd. These elements are the factors in the teacher's core nature that make him or her outstanding. Patience, respect, forgiveness, and love guide planning and preparation for students every day of every year. Patience, respect, forgiveness, and love empower classroom management techniques and characterize every interchange with students.

The Golden Rule classroom management plan is simply an implementation of a traditional maxim—the Golden Rule itself (Bible, book of Matthew 7:12). In other words, treat students as you would like to be treated if you were a student. Interact with students in patterns you would like if you were a student. It is really just that simple. What about the students who do not know correct behavior, who have such crises in their lives that they cannot separate right from wrong? Consider: If you had been born into difficult circumstances, how would you have wanted your teacher to handle you, interact with you, respond to your inappropriate language, and stimulate your confidence to overcome fear of failure? Surely, the answer is the Golden Rule answer: patience, respect, forgiveness, and love—endless love!

Effective Teachers Operate on the Golden Rule

Overall, a teacher must recognize some basic principles for effective classroom management. Effective teachers have reasonable rules, expectations, or responsibility statements that set limits and define appropriate conduct. Appropriate conduct leads to active student participation, learning success, and high achievement. Effective teachers post rules or expectations and refer to them frequently, making them a clearly important element in the classroom culture. Effective teachers identify appropriate rewards and consequences relative to expectations. Effective teachers create efficient procedures that facilitate student learning and accomplishment. Effective teachers demonstrate and model respect for individual learners. Effective teachers usually involve learners in defining the expectations for the classroom. Effective teachers use the Golden Rule approach in developing class management strategies—that is, they do not ask learners anything that they would not want asked of themselves, were they among the students in a class. Effective teachers always keep their eyes focused on the goal: enhanced student learning.

CLASSROOM ENVIRONMENT AND ORGANIZATION

The classroom layout can also influence student conduct and responses during lessons. Careful thought about where to place the resources that students must routinely access is essential when setting up the classroom. I can report about one highly experienced social studies middle grade teacher who was reputed to have chaotic classrooms. One look in her room revealed some causes of the chaotic environment. She had all of her student desks placed in rows so tightly together that students had to, quite literally, walk across the tops of them to get to the desks nearest the wall. Her own desk and counter space, plus much of the floor, were piled high with old class projects from years gone by, old out-of-date textbooks, and a lot of useless material that should have long ago gone into the trash. She had student resources placed in a corner near her desk, but that desk was piled so high with papers and paraphernalia that the necessary materials were covered over because piles had fallen on them. Students had to plow through these fallen piles of papers to find the textbooks, dictionaries, and other classroom resources needed for lesson activities.

In addition to giving this teacher some simple classroom conduct standards and procedures in a discipline plan, we had to, quite literally, dig out her classroom and create space in which it would be possible for students to learn. It was not that she had too many students, she just had too much stuff! How can the classroom be arranged so that the room itself becomes a tool for effective learning? Where would be the most efficient place to place materials that students will access? How much space is necessary around students so that they are not inadvertently invading each other's space? How can desks be clustered to create more open space? When we discuss cooperative learning strategies, we will make the case that placing students facing each other creates an irresistible urge to communicate because we are social beings. There are times when this is necessary and important, and then there are other times. How can you face the students so that they can easily and quickly change position when they need to be facing the teacher for teacher-directed learning? These questions will be useful to the new teacher or the classroom veteran when planning for new academic terms or school years.

Of course, who among the ranks of teachers has not had to face the reality of excessive enrollment and limited space? Both state laws and teacher contract provisions delimit the number of children who may be placed in a room with a given amount of space. Our creative efforts to accommodate burgeoning enrollments should always be accompanied with professional wisdom about just how many bodies and desks can be placed in the floor space available. Then we can creatively design arrangements to maximize the uses of that space and the learning environment.

Another distinction between the rookie and the effective veteran is the use of display items. Some teachers may just decorate their classrooms with hanging fish, pictures, colorful paper, and so on. Some may so extensively decorate the room that it stimulates confusion and emotional reactions among many students who may be more sensitive to such stimuli. Effective teachers, however, will use the room as a teaching tool. Displays will be related to the content currently being delivered and will be arranged so that students can focus on them but not be distracted by them. Displays will be learning reinforcements that help the students as they master skills and information. They will be attractive, possibly soothing, and definitely not cluttered. They will also reflect the personality of the teacher and the emerging personality of the collective class.

The display area will include spaces that the students can use to celebrate their successful efforts. Student work will be prominent among the classroom display environment.

BUILDING A COMMUNITY OF LEARNING

The classroom should be seen as a community for learning in which students, as well as the teacher, are citizens. I can still see one of the master teachers I worked with when I started teaching many decades ago as she announced to her students (and to me, the bright-eyed student teacher) that this classroom was a "queendom." She was its queen, and they were all her subjects. I remember thinking that I was surprised she didn't require them all to call her "your majesty," but she didn't go quite that far. Times have changed, and such pronouncements by teachers today will be met with jeers and cynicism by students who are generations removed from any sort of automatic respect for authority, due just because of one's station or role. In today's classroom, the teacher is a servant, serving children by molding their dreams and equipping them for success. It is a place students should think of as safe and comfortable, while at the same time a place of learning and engagement. This tone is established not only by the environment but also by the teacher's attitude about the students; both will add to or detract from this evolving learning community.

A Teacher's Experience:
Jan Gannon's Classroom Community

Janet Gannon, the 2003 North Carolina Teacher of the Year, taught at an elementary school in North Carolina for 5 years. Jan has created a Web site to share her rich heritage for teaching excellence and many resources (see Gannon, 2003).

Jan seeks to create classroom community with several exciting strategies.

- Teasing, name calling, and so on are forbidden. We work on using kind words at all times. I express to the children that we might not all be best friends, but we are all friends. We think about the words we say before we say them. We work on disagreeing in a way that is not hurtful to others.
- I treat my students with respect and courtesy, and I expect the same from them.
- Class officers are elected and have real responsibilities.
- I encourage interaction among the students, and I provide opportunities for "peer teaching" on a daily basis.
- Every child has a job. (They can be relieved of their duty in extreme circumstances.) There are fun and "not-so-fun" jobs that need to be done each day. The jobs change weekly.

- Children work together to solve their own conflicts by using "I Messages."
- Children have input when it comes to the curriculum. (I usually provide appropriate choices, and I let them make the decision.)
- Students are given choices as much as possible and are encouraged to really "think" throughout the day.
- My lessons are student-centered rather than teacher-centered. I try to keep students as actively involved as possible. Even the most traditional lessons can become engaging when a child is teaching! Note: Some of my units are posted online.
- We have "share time" on a daily basis. This is a five-minute period in which a child shares something from home, a story they have written, or an experience with the class. He/she takes questions and comments from the class. (Children sign up in advance.)
- We have "story time" every day after share time. While I read aloud from a novel, the children must be quiet. However, they can draw, color, write, or work on missing work at their desks as I read. They cherish this time for themselves.
- I hold private behavior conferences on an as-needed basis. I never embarrass my students by putting their names on the board. (See class rules.) In addition, the children can schedule appointments with me to discuss private issues that concern them. I usually do these conferences at lunch.
- I let the children really "know" me. If you asked one of my students to tell you about me, they would say that I love cheese, movies, and dogs. They would also tell you that I don't like unkind words, lying, and bananas. They know that I really want to be there, and I think that is half the battle!
- I am silly! We can laugh and joke together as a family while meeting our academic goals. I am learning, too!
- They don't have to ask permission to go to the bathroom. As long as we are not in the middle of a lesson, they know that they can go without asking. If they abuse the privilege, they lose it. Then, they have to raise their hand for everything. They usually work hard to be responsible. (Of course, I am able to do this because I have a bathroom and water fountain in my room.)
- I try to never use the words "My Classroom." It's OUR classroom. I AM the authority figure in the room, but I also want to be seen as part of the classroom family. (Gannon, 2003)

Jan offers six suggestions for classroom behavior standards for herself as a teacher-servant.

1. Be fair and consistent at all times. Make sure that you don't have any teacher's pets.

2. Follow through! If you say you are going to do something, do it!

3. Provide a student-centered learning environment in which students can become engaged in the learning process. You will find that your number of behavior problems goes down as the level of student engagement goes up.

4. Be a role model. Work together to solve conflicts. Be patient. Have a sense of humor. Model a positive attitude towards school and learning.

5. Be yourself! Don't be afraid to let them know that you care!

6. Work hard to develop a positive home/school relationship! (Gannon, 2003)

When teachers see themselves with, as Parker Palmer (1993) puts it, a teacher's heart, then they see themselves as willing to do anything and everything to make a difference in the lives of the learners they serve. Jan is certainly one such teacher with a teacher's heart! Classrooms with community-building principles such as Jan's will always make dreams possible and futures successful for the pupils who are fortunate enough to live in them.

3

Designing Learning
Experiences

Guiding Questions

1. What is an instructional objective?
2. How is an instructional objective created for effective learning outcomes?
3. How might an effective teacher make use of cognitive, psychomotor, and affective taxonomies for creating instructional objectives or outcomes?
4. Who is the ultimate author of each student's learning plan? Why?
5. What is the connection of instructional objectives, learning outcomes, and overall assessment of school effectiveness?
6. How might the General Model for Teaching help my instructional planning and development of effective teaching objectives?

As explained in the first chapter, effective teachers plan instruction that draws on and values students' backgrounds, prior knowledge, and interests. Teachers establish challenging learning goals for all students based on student experience, language, and development, home, and school expectations. Teachers sequence curriculum and design short-term and long-term plans that incorporate subject matter knowledge, reflect grade-level curriculum expectations, and include a repertoire of instructional strategies. Teachers use instructional activities that promote learning goals and connect with student experiences and interests. Teachers modify and adjust instructional plans according to student engagement and achievement.

Have you ever sat in a class or a meeting and thought to yourself: What am I doing here? Two questions that learners of all time have asked themselves are: What are we doing here?—followed by: Why do I need to know this? Effective teachers find ways to answer these questions early in a lesson. Those questions are addressed at some point, both generally and specifically, regardless of the particular model of lesson design.

To answer these questions, the teacher must have an *instructional objective.* Given an objective, the student knows the expected task, the criteria for a successful outcome, and the personal meaning and importance of this particular learning. Although the notion of instructional objectives was most precisely formulated in connection with behavioral models of teaching and learning, instructional objectives can be modified to focus lesson design in any of the several models presented later in this book.

TEACHING THAT TARGETS LEARNING

All teaching is derived from general goals. Students are expected to become knowledgeable in certain areas of life. To this end, goals are established by society and by experts in various fields of endeavor, as well as by learners themselves. Thus, these goals are processed by many different entities prior to becoming classroom instructional objectives. Moreover, multiple theories exist to explain how the learning process actually takes place. People attempting to answer questions about readiness, stages of development behavioral responses to stimuli, and individual meaning suggest various approaches to conducting a learning activity and may even look for different evidence of the accomplished learning. Because there are many different orientations, or approaches, to the teaching-learning process, similar goals may have very different appearances when applied to classroom instruction.

Generally speaking, several objectives are derived from a single goal. For example, a goal that students will *learn to read* may generate an extensive series of objectives. Those objectives are arranged in a particular sequence designed to produce mastery of reading skills. Such objectives may be *cognitive, psychomotor,* or *affective* in nature. Most objectives in classroom learning are cognitive, although a number are attitudinal, or affective. An objective should be expressed to reflect the domain of learning and should indicate the anticipated outcome.

The Cognitive Taxonomy

Cognition is the act in which learners think about information, ideas, and other input, then process that material into action or anticipated action. Benjamin Bloom (1956) has outlined progressive levels of cognitive activity proceeding from information through knowledge, comprehension or understanding, application, analysis, and synthesis to evaluation. According to most theorists and practitioners, the vast majority of current teaching activity aims at the knowledge and comprehension levels. We seem to want to spend more time giving learners information and then helping them understand its meaning. Consequently, we spend little time helping them to know what to do with that information. Here are the learner's activities at each of Bloom's six cognitive levels.

Bloom's Taxonomy

Level 6	Evaluation	Makes judgments; offers opinions
Level 5	Synthesis	Makes predictions, produces original communications, or solves problems
Level 4	Analysis	Identifies motives or causes, draws conclusions, or determines evidence
Level 3	Application	Applies knowledge to determine an appropriate, correct answer
Level 2	Comprehension	Rephrases, rewords, and compares information
Level 1	Knowledge	Demonstrates memory only; repeats information exactly as memorized

Thus, when taught at *knowledge* levels, the learner remembers specific facts or ideas, terms, patterns, or settings. Expectations focus on recall and data retrieval. At *comprehension* levels, the learner is led to understand whatever is presented by means of simple, repeated explanations. Moving up the scale to *application* requires that learners remember, understand, and make use of ideas, rules, or other data, first in a known situation and then, perhaps, in unfamiliar situations. A still higher-level objective is *analysis*. Learners disassemble and examine the components of a concept, a set of facts, a collection of information, or the like and classify the elements in some organized way for future communication. At the next level, *synthesis*, objectives ask learners to take information that has been analyzed and reassemble it, perhaps in some original or unique way, to solve a problem, overcome a challenge, or resolve an issue. The highest level of Bloom's cognitive taxonomy, *evaluation*, asks learners to judge an idea, abstraction, problem solution, or other learning according to given or personally developed criteria.

Good teaching calls on learners to work their way upward on this taxonomic scale. Figure 3.1 suggests several activities and objectives built around a theme of flight, demonstrating increasingly higher order objectives.

The Psychomotor Taxonomy

Different individuals have varying degrees of physical ability; some abilities are learned, and others are apparently related to genetic development. Characteristics such as body type and physical health of all sensory organs—especially hearing and balance, vision, and perception—relate to physical performance. Bloom (1956) has developed a psychomotor taxonomy with six

Figure 3.1   Objectives in the Cognitive Taxonomy

Taxonomy Level	1. How does nature fly?	2. How and why do people fly?	3. Who flies?
6 Evaluation	Determine the most effective flying creatures		
5 Synthesis	Create a story involving flying creatures		Write a biography of a fictional flying hero of the future
4 Analysis	Compare and contrast naturally flying creatures	Compare past flight with modern flight	
3 Application	Identify that natural creatures fly	Illustrate the principles as they apply to space flight	List modern-day counterparts to such fliers
2 Comprehension	Explain the basic principle in natural flight	Explain the flight of balloons, jets, and gliders	Read a biography of a famous fliers
1 Knowledge	Identify birds' flight patterns	List the principles of aerodynamics	

levels: reflex movements, basic fundamental movements, perceptual abilities, physical abilities, skilled movements, and nondiscursive communication. Harrow (1972) suggests that progressive psychomotor development must transition from simple to complex and from external to internal controls. Instructional objectives in the psychomotor area would accomplish the following levels of performance:

Psychomotor Taxonomy

Level 6	Nondiscursive communication	Use our bodies to express feelings or ideas
Level 5	Skilled movements	Complex physical skills like rope-jumping or shooting basketballs through the basket
Level 4	Physical abilities	Development of strength, endurance, flexibility, and agility
Level 3	Perceptual abilities	Permit the coordination of muscle movements in response to the outside world through sensory feedback
Level 2	Fundamental movements	Behaviors learned in the early years like grasping, walking, and so on, which form the foundation for later growth and physical development
Level 1	Reflex movements	Behaviors outside the conscious control of the learner, like breathing, protecting, or shielding from incoming objects; reflex actions from touching something hot or painful

Physical education objectives are most often tied to this taxonomy, although drama, dance, music, and other nonverbal communication subjects will also frame objectives according to this language. A dance teacher might have as a goal: Students will develop expressive movements with hands and arms to communicate specific thought. An instrumental music teacher might use an objective for preparing concert presentations: Students will reflect the music in their physical movements as they are playing. As in the cognitive taxonomy, these levels are cumulative. Students must learn *reflex movement* in preparation for *fundamental movement*. Both of those lead the physical learner into *perceptual abilities* or control over the body's responses. *Physical abilities* flow out of these lower order developments and lead the individual into controlled *physical ability*. *Skilled movements* are the next level of developed physical ability. A well-developed individual is prepared for lifelong use of *nondiscursive communication* skills to aid in personal physical expressiveness.

The Affective Taxonomy

Krathwohl, Bloom, and Masia (1964) provided a taxonomy of teaching levels within the affective domain. Affective objectives are concerned with student attitudes about content. Objectives in this area of learning focus on learners' personal values and valuing processes as demonstrated by their *willingness* to do certain things, rather than their *ability* to do them. This taxonomy is organized into five levels:

Affective Taxonomy

Level 5	Characterization by value	Learners internalize ideas in ways that lead them to consciously modify personal behaviors
Level 4	Organization	Learners arrange ideas into a system or rationale to apply to future decisions about personal actions or behaviors
Level 3	Valuing	Learners make a personal commitment and assume responsibility for a particular response to information presented
Level 2	Responding	Learners show a personal willingness to respond to ideas, suggestions, or other information
Level 1	Attending or receiving	Learners accept information, albeit passively, with little or no direct or immediate response

Initially, then, learners accept information, albeit passively, with little or no direct or immediate response. As they reach the third level, valuing, learners make a personal commitment and assume some responsibility for their response to the information presented. Emotion begins to play a part as learners identify personally with the information and stake out, with varying degrees of passion, a personal position. At Levels 3 through 5, students indicate levels of value. Students achieve appreciation when they recognize the information is of personal worth. They arrange ideas into a system or rationale to apply to future actions or behaviors. They achieve task-undertaking value when they willingly and consciously choose to modify personal behaviors, to attempt tasks or activities, even at some personal risk.

WRITING INSTRUCTIONAL OBJECTIVES

Good teachers are always aware of the outcomes that lessons are intended to produce in learners. They may be looking for cognitive outcomes, psychomotor outcomes, or affective outcomes. Often, two or all three areas may intertwine. Teachers should consider what *ought* to occur and what they would like to see demonstrated, then judge whether the outcome falls in one, two, or all three domains of learning. With that decision made, teachers formulate objectives to describe the desired outcomes as observable or measurable behaviors. The affective domain is the most difficult to observe or measure accurately. That is, affective outcomes are *squishy* in that they are hard to identify or observe from one day to the next, from person to person, from teacher to teacher. They are a lot like the proverbial problem of nailing Jell-O to the wall because their consistent confirmation is nearly impossible. Therefore, objectives in this area may be left to secondary, or indirect, confirmation. That leaves us to formulate behavioral objectives in the cognitive or psychomotor domain. More often, the emphasis falls on the cognitive domain.

Good observable objectives are, most often, *behavioral* because we can directly observe the results in the learners' performances and demonstrations. Four simple elements result in an instructional objective:

- Describe the subject matter content
- Specify the general goals
- Break down the general educational goals into more specific, observable objectives
- Word the objectives for clarity and appropriateness

Often, in their planning, teachers accomplish Elements 1 and 2 for an entire semester or year, while Elements 3 and 4 are repeated for every lesson. A useful format for an objective is exemplified here. It identifies the learner and content area, then the specific taxonomic level of thinking and performance outcome.

How to State an Objective

Identify the learner and content area	The student in eighth-grade humanities class will . . .
Identify the specific taxonomic level of thinking and performance outcome	. . . **construct** a comparison chart of the causes of the Civil War from both a Northern and a Southern perspective, citing appropriate historically accurate sources. **or** . . . **demonstrate *analysis*** of the causes of the Civil War **by constructing** a comparison chart citing both Northern and Southern perspectives taken from historically accurate sources.

Instructional outcome is in the verb

The verbs in an objective are particularly important because they identify the activity and the level of performance. Many teachers struggle with vague or unobservable verbs in their objectives, for example: "Students will learn about multiplication." *Learn about* is a vague concept. Learn *what* about multiplication? How will I *see* that students have learned it? Verbs such as *know, enjoy, understand, familiarize, comprehend, value, grasp, realize, believe, like, appreciate, cope with, think,* and *love* are generally too imprecise to delineate what is expected of the student.

Much preferred are verbs that describe observable actions—or actions that yield observable products. Verbs like *identify, analyze, speak, predict, list, locate, select, explain, choose, isolate, compute, divide, add, separate, draw,* or *infer* are much more useful in wording instructional objectives. They enable both teacher and student to recognize successful learning once it has been achieved.

Many processes and skills that cannot be directly observed nevertheless produce observable products. In such cases it is acceptable to identify the product of the lesson, presuming that the learner must master the process to create the product. As in the objective above from a unit on the Civil War, the process target of the objective is the ability to think analytically, to dissect the causes of the Civil War, and to compare two different views of such causes. In creating the chart comparing the two regional views, the student is presumed to have *compared and contrasted* the various causal issues from two different viewpoints. Thus, the objective should read: Students in the eighth-grade humanities class will *demonstrate analysis* of the causes of the Civil War *by constructing* a comparison chart citing both *Northern and Southern* perspectives taken from historically accurate sources.

An instructional objective emphasizes what the student is expected to do, not what the teacher will do. New teachers who are asked to state the objective of a lesson may respond with "to present multiplication facts," or some similar statement. But the objective should not be to *present* multiplication facts—that the teacher does—but to *know, understand, apply, analyze, synthesize,* or *evaluate* multiplication facts—that students do. The teacher's delivery activity may be presenting the facts; the teacher may also motivate learners; but neither is a correct objective for a lesson. There is no accountability for the student in an objective that calls merely for presentation or other action by the teacher. Some correctly worded objectives, in both short and long form, are suggested here.

Words That Embody Objectives

Students will solve long-division problems using at least two different methods.

OR

Students will demonstrate application of long division by correctly solving problems using two different methods.

Students will list the five punctuation rules discussed in the text.

OR

Students will demonstrate knowledge of punctuation rules by listing them.

Students will correctly complete two-decimal division problems.

OR

Students will demonstrate understanding of two-decimal division by completion of assigned problems.

Students will develop and follow a story outline in writing a story.

OR

Students will demonstrate synthesis of the writing process elements by correctly developing and following a plan to write a story.

Figure 3.2 lists verbs and other key words matched to the levels in Bloom's cognitive taxonomy.

ASSESSMENT OF LEARNING OUTCOMES

When teachers plan for teaching, they consider what the learner ought to know, as determined by subject matter experts, society, and to some degree the learners themselves. Then, the teacher prepares plans for delivering content that is based on quality standards for learning, which have been prescribed by

Figure 3.2   Verbs and Key Words for the Cognitive Taxonomy

Cognitive Taxonomy Terms:

Knowledge	define, recall, recognize, remember, who, what, where, when
Comprehension	describe, compare, contrast, rephrase, put into your own words, explain
Application	apply, classify, use, choose, employ, write an example of, solve, how many, which, what is
Analysis	identify motives or causes, draw conclusions, determine evidence, support, analyze, why
Synthesis	predict, produce, write, design, develop, synthesize, construct, create, improve upon, what if? devise, create solutions
Evaluation	judge, argue, decide, evaluate, assess, give your opinion, determine which is better, agree or disagree

Source: Adapted from Krathwohl et al. (1964).

the several state educational agencies and the national organizations for educational content learning. The key next element for the teacher is to make continuous assessment of individual students' learning. What have they learned to date? What is yet needed? Are they equipped to handle the next planned element in the chain of their learning?

Effective teachers need to be able to make an initial assessment of each student's status in the several domains of learning under the teacher's tutelage. What does the student know in contrast to what he or she needs to know at this particular point in the learning sequence? What is the student's preferred learning style? How shall the next learning elements be packaged and delivered? This initial assessment is not so different from the diagnosis made by a medical professional considering a patient who appears to be in need of some sort of treatment. The teacher's diagnosis, then, leads to professional decisions about the treatment to be given to the learner. One problem with education reform at the national level in the middle of the first decade in the 21st century is that policymakers are erroneously attempting to prescribe teaching technique along with content.

Not even the most knowledgeable content expert could begin to design truly effective and appropriate learning delivery strategies for all children across the United States of America, sight unseen! The states are too diverse. The people are too diverse. The languages are too diverse. The needs of the individuals are too diverse. Even within a given educational district boundary, the diversity is such that scripted curriculum is, perhaps, the largest of the educational reform follies. It has failed in the past and will fail again and again because it removes the important diagnostician role for the teacher on the ground and in front of the learners. Only an effective teacher, after thoughtful reflection about each individual learner's demonstrated need, can make an accurate decision about the appropriate educational treatment to correct the educational deficiency or to extend the educational mastery.

Thus, teachers must be well equipped to assess learning needs. This skill comes through a thorough knowledge of the subjects and content to be taught and from the teacher's comparison of students' demonstrations of understanding and application with that thorough knowledge.

Backward Mapping

Effective teachers look at what knowledge individual learners making up their class need, and then at what each actually knows. Teachers then proceed to design down from that ultimate outcome until they arrive at the point where each individual learner is at present. In the planning process, teachers usually ask questions such as: What does this learner need to know to demonstrate mastery? What does the learner need to know to learn the final clue to mastery? What does he or she need to acquire that clue? And so the query leads backward to the place where the student now stands waiting to be led and encouraged along a learning path. If learning outcomes were a hike, the teacher would start at the end of the trail and walk it backward to discover the obstacles and interesting points along the way that can be used or must be mitigated in the educational design.

In planning for the academic year's learning activities, each teacher will want to identify the skills and abilities needed by students as they leave their classrooms and enter the next grade level. How would the teacher want each pupil to be equipped if he or she were to be the teacher at that next level? Working back from that picture, the teacher then can sketch a sequence of learning outcome mastery descriptions that every learner can attain. Teachers work back to the point at which the academic year begins, but they must think not only of the average or ideal beginning student. The reality is that of the several students, many will be below the desirable level of preparation, so teachers should think back to the beginning of, perhaps, the previous grade level and ask themselves "what-if" questions: What if one of my students reads two years below the present normal grade-level expectation? How will I help him to catch up rapidly? What if one or more of the children I serve have learning handicaps? How will I be able to adjust their learning activities so that they acquire necessary skills and abilities to go on?

Nationally noted expert on educational design Grant Wiggins (2002) was recently asked to describe why it is important for teachers to consider assessment strategies prior to planning their lessons and learning projects:

> One of the challenges in teaching is designing, and to be a good designer you have to think about what you're trying to accomplish and craft a combination of the content and the instructional methods, but also the assessment. And one of the things that we've done over the last years in working with teachers is share with them how important it is to say, "What are you going to assess? What's evidence of the goals that you have in mind?" Otherwise your teaching can end up being hit or miss. We call it backward design. Instead of jumping to the activities—"Oh I could have kids do this, oh, that'd be cool"—you say, "Well, wait a minute, wait a minute." Before you decide exactly what you're going to do with them, if you achieve your objective, what does it look like? What's the evidence

that they got it? What's the evidence that they can now do it, whatever the "it" is? So you have to think about how it's going to end up, what it's going to look like. And then that ripples back into your design, what activities will get you there. What teaching moves will get you there?

Another good explanation of this design-down thinking can be seen in a discussion by Larry Ainsworth (2003) in *Power Standards: Identifying the Standards That Matter Most.* This book discusses assessment strategies, but designing one's curriculum for an upcoming academic term certainly involves actual assessment of the real abilities, strengths, and needs of the real pupils a teacher has sitting in the classroom. Perhaps one of Ainsworth's most revealing discussions is in Chapter 2, where he describes an interaction with teaching staff during a series of training sessions. He asked them to identify the geometry principles that were taught for mastery at each grade level. The intent was to put the principles up on the wall and discuss their alignment with standards and curriculum content materials. What he discovered, however, was that none of the primary teachers taught anything related to geometry at all, and that it was not until the fourth grade that pupils began to receive instruction in this subskill area of mathematics. The problem was that the state testing required fourth graders to be proficient with certain geometry principles, but they could not all be covered by the fourth-grade teachers along with all the rest of their curriculum. Ainsworth asked the whole staff whether the geometry portion of the state exam was a fourth-grade test only or a kindergarten through fourth-grade assessment. The teachers all realized that it was the latter, and soon, discussion began on how teachers below Grade 4 could identify appropriate geometry skills to prepare children for what needed to be covered in their fourth-grade math lessons. This is a design-down way of thinking about mastery teaching.

THE GENERAL MODEL FOR TEACHING

The literature about teaching includes broad discussion of models, strategies, and methods. As a result, teachers and teacher educators have identified a considerable number of these models and methods as consistent with effective teaching practice. Such models, as we shall see, serve as source patterns on which creative teachers draw to invent meaningful lessons, rather than as precise prescriptions or canned strategies. They all fit a general plan for teaching that could be called the General Model for Teaching. This generalized understanding of instruction, like all other models, is presented here as a reference for analyzing all lessons, regardless of their source models—not as an exact prescription to be replicated by teachers.

Planning occurs in four elements: (1) preparation and planning, (2) framing the lesson, (3) instructional input and learning, and (4) integration of the learning for insight and clarification. This process is outlined below. It is important in this and all use of models or patterns for lesson design that the teacher has clear understanding of envisioned learning outcomes, what they look like in actual student performances, and how they equip the student to move into the next level. Before designing the first lesson, as was discussed earlier, effective teachers go to the end and carefully understand the ultimate outcome. Then, the planning takes place, and the lesson design takes shape.

Element 1: Preparation and Planning

- Diagnose student need
- Construct learning objective
- Select model(s) and strategy(ies)
- Consider possible tasks and activities
- Select tasks and activities

Element 2: Framing the Lesson

- Link to previous understanding
- Establish purposive focus and level of concern
- Prepare procedural directions

Element 3: Instructional Delivery and Learning

- Select instructional media and delivery forms for presentation of content
- Plan activities to monitor and adjust for understanding and task acquisition
- Plan procedures for motivation and reinforcement

Questions, sequences of questions, probes, prompts, and piggy-back responses are tools the teacher uses to evaluate the level of successful thought about and application of each component of the learning that students are experiencing. In a sense, each subcomponent idea or notion must reach closure; that is to say, it must be applied and owned by the learner in a meaningful way. With well-arranged questions, the teacher can do this.

Element 4: Integration of the Learning for Insight and Clarification

In leading, directing, or facilitating a student's discovery, understanding, or application of the learning in question, the teacher facilitates integration of the new knowledge into existing patterns of understanding.

STRUCTURE OF THE LEARNING CLIMATE

The purpose of the General Model for Teaching is to establish a generally applicable frame of reference for the teacher in *all* teaching situations. It is a model of models. It includes all the other models, from low to high structure. Suffice it to say that the teacher makes a conscious decision about the level of structure necessary in each lesson and applies techniques, strategies, and activities to establish the desired structure.

Teacher/Learner Interaction

How will the teacher interact with students? The teacher makes this decision based on the focus, the model components used, a task analysis, and a diagnosis of student need. Will the teacher direct the learner from point to point and from key idea to key idea? Will the teacher use questioning strategies to direct the learners' attention? Will the teacher serve as facilitator and guide—or as the source of knowledge and wisdom? Will the teacher motivate and reinforce learners with positive responses, encouraging comments and stretching challenges? Motivation is a factor the teacher must consider in any lesson, any model or method. The teacher must establish and maintain an appropriate level of concern among students at every stage or element in a lesson. In other words, care must be taken not to *over*whelm students, but not to "*under*whelm" them either. The information, concept, or skill to be taught, and each component element or stage of teaching it, must seem to the learners to be worthy of their attention.

Outcomes

Outcomes are achieved directly by leading learners in particular directions. Outcomes are both instructional and nurturing, but the degree of emphasis on instruction or nurture varies across the several model components that a teacher may decide to use. On the following page is a planning sheet (Figure 3.3) that teachers may use in planning lessons in the General Model for Teaching.

The General Model is offered here to satisfy the zeal of some to force a particular model or notorious method into a generalizable plan. It is not really suggested that all teachers must take this simple outline and begin to plug into it all such things as may be desired, though it certainly could be used in that way. Teachers are encouraged to take this model as a suggested starting place and then apply professional creativity to meet the assessed needs of their learners.

SUMMARY

Effective teaching requires teachers to pay careful attention to learning design. They must have a great vision about what the effective learning outcome will look like when successfully achieved and then work backward from that vision as the learning activities are created and the learning materials are selected. Accurate learning objectives or outcomes require teachers to clarify the subject matter and decide whether the learning will take place in the psychomotor, cognitive, or affective domain or in a combination of domains. Next, the carefully worded objective should identify: *Who?* and *What will be done?* At what thought level will the student process the material? How will success be demonstrated?

The evaluation of learning hinges on the ability to observe authentic learning outcomes. The key to an observable objective is an observable verb. When teachers develop instructional objectives for their teaching, they must watch the verbs! When teachers develop the lesson design, they must envision outcome connected to the string of development that leads to successful learning

Figure 3.3   The General Teaching Model Planning Sheet

Element 1: Preparation and Planning

Student Need	Learning Objective	Appropriate Models and Strategy(ies)	Possible Tasks and Activities	Tasks and Activities

Element 2: Framing the Lesson

Links to Previous Understanding	Purposive Focus and Level of Concern	Procedural Directions

Element 3: Instructional Delivery and Learning

Media and Formats to Deliver Content	Activities for Monitoring and Adjusting	Motivation and Reinforcement Procedures
	Understanding Task Acquisition Level of Concern	

Element 4: Integration of the Learning for Insight and Clarification

performances by students. It is up to excellent teachers to empower pupils to demonstrate that they are ready for their next level of learning. This means that teachers plan with both the grade-level end and the cumulative end of the learning years in mind, regardless of the subject or the grade level in which the learning is being offered. Drawing back to national standards for teaching effectiveness, we want to remember that, as a standard for excellence, "Teachers *think* systematically about their practice and *learn* from experience" (NBPT Proposition 4).

A major key to such systematic thought is the careful analysis of student needs, careful development of lesson plans designed to address those needs, and careful attention or reflection on the level of learning outcome effectiveness accomplished for use in future planning and preparation. The remaining chapters of this book are designed to provide teachers and instructional leaders with models, methods, and strategies for teaching effectively and making the decisions teachers must make in designing learning environments.

4

The Behavioral Models

Guiding Questions

1. What is implied about teaching and learning by the term *direct instruction*, and how does the model work?

2. What is an *advance organizer*, and how can it be used to enhance learning outcomes?

3. How many different ways can the *memory model* or its components be used for effective learning outcomes?

4. What is *mastery learning*, and how can effective teachers make use of its ideas?

5. If you were to create a method based on the *mastery lecture method*, what might it look like?

The models, methods, and strategies discussed in this chapter are termed *behavioral models*. Why is that so? Is it important to understand why when designing learning activities? Why?

Drawing heavily from the studies of Skinner, Thorndike, Pavlov, and many others in behavioral psychology, behavioral models enjoy varying degrees of use in classrooms today. Modern behavioral theory cites relationships between stimuli and resulting effects of operant conditioning and counterconditioning. In the models derived from the behavioral stance, we find the following elements:

- Stimulus control
- Generalization and discrimination
- Response repertoires and response substitution
- Reinforcers and reinforcement schedules
- Observation, modeling, and practice

Types of mastery behavioral models have been presented in the research on teaching under various names and in slightly modified formats. *Direct instruction, mastery learning, advance organizer, practice theory,* and *memory models,* along with the *mastery lecture method,* are discussed in the following pages as examples.

DIRECT INSTRUCTION

Direct instruction, as a teaching model, draws from the research on mastery learning and practice theory. It presumes a highly behaviorist view of learning through reinforcement. The instructional design includes task analysis, which separates a learning task into subcomponents, each of which is to be explained and demonstrated. The teacher monitors or checks the progressive understanding of students as they proceed through a lesson. Nonacademic materials and interactions are discouraged during learning experiences. Lessons are objective based and sequentially arranged so as to cumulate to a larger concept or skill. The various strategies of direct instruction draw from the work of Barak Rosenshine, Madeline Hunter, and other behavioral psychologists.

This term *direct instruction* suggests a pattern in which the teacher

- Explains new concepts or skills to the whole group
- Tests students' understanding by practice under teacher direction and monitoring (controlled practice)
- Encourages students to continue to practice semi-independently in the classroom (guided practice)

In the past 30 years, direct instruction has been popularized by proponents of the work of Dr. Madeline Hunter and the Laboratory School at the University of California, Los Angeles. In this model, the above elements are bracketed by an extensively detailed *anticipatory set* and *independent practice.* The anticipatory set relates to previous learning and presents the objective of the current lesson. Input involves the teacher's explanations, including presentations with any and all media. The teacher monitors student performance and adjusts the experience to ensure maximum success as learners progress through the planned lesson. In direct instruction, the teacher systematically transfers an idea to the students, first demonstrating, then asking students to assist in the demonstration, then asking students to attempt demonstration as the teacher provides assistance, and finally requiring students to make successful demonstration in *independent practice.* This sequence has been popularized as:

- I (the teacher) do it.
- You (the learner) help me do it.
- I help you do it.
- You do it alone.

A major variation of the Hunter model includes an element called *closure.* The concept of closure was not part of the original Hunter-Russell model, but it has been added by proponents of the model over time (Ehrgott & Luehe, 1984). Closure was originally intended to suggest that the teacher would verify complete understanding by each student before proceeding to the next piece of the learning—a final monitoring or check for understanding. Closure became linked over time and application with the notion of summarizing and completing a lesson with a final monitoring activity. The idea of closure is that the teacher must verify, before the conclusion of the class session, that each learner has indeed acquired the intended learning. Certainly, pupils should not be sent home to complete homework without such an element, or they risk practicing errors rather than correctly learned skills and knowledge.

The closure of a lesson summarizes, restates the objective, verifies the learning, and sets a tone for the next learning session. However, although closure is included here, it may not be essential. The question is whether a particular application warrants a final summarization or refocusing on the accomplished objective. Some theorists and practitioners in the field suggest that closure is better practiced within each element, rather than as a separate element or element of the direct instruction model. That is to say, the teacher should "get closure" on each key concept presented.

Some, including Hunter herself (1989), suggest that the Hunter-Russell model and other versions of direct instruction may have been misapplied and oversimplified by instructional leaders who did not have sufficient pedagogical breadth to maintain appropriate perspective. Once implemented, however, direct instruction has been a preferred model among teachers and administrators because of its understandable system and the positive short-term results that it appears to yield. Among the many models available to teachers, direct instruction, properly implemented, is particularly effective for teaching skills.

The model is presented below in five elements, although in the literature it is found in several different formats. All these are simply different clustering of the 13 components of direct instruction shown below. Next, we discuss the plan, necessary structure, teacher/learner interaction, and outcomes of direct instruction.

The Plan

Planning for direct instruction occurs in four elements: (1) orientation (anticipatory set), (2) teaching input and monitoring understanding, (3) closure, and (4) independent practice. This process is outlined next.

13 Components of Direct Instruction

Preparation
Diagnosis
Anticipatory set
Relevance to previous learning and appropriate level of concern
Statement of objective
Input/instruction
Modeling
Monitoring/checking for understanding
Guided practice
Closure (Marshall, 2003)
Independent practice
Evaluation
Remediation

Element 1: Orientation (Anticipatory Set)

The teacher will want to engage the learners through short, clear, and meaningful statements that

- Establish the content of the lesson
- Review previous learning
- Establish lesson objectives
- Establish procedures for the lesson

Element 2: Teaching Input and Monitoring Understanding

Without particular sequence, the teacher will model, monitor student learning, and guide their practice, freely moving among these three activities as needed.

Modeling

- Explain or demonstrate the new concept or skill
- Provide visual representation of the task

Monitoring

- Check all students for understanding
- Determine the degree to which each is on track for mastering the desired learning

Guiding practice

- Lead the group through practice examples in lock element (I do it)
- Have students respond to questions (You help me do it)
- Provide corrective feedback on errors and reinforce correct practice (I help you do it)

- Have students practice semi-independently (You do it)
- Provide feedback
- Circulate, monitoring student practice

Element 3: Closure

To gather the students' thinking and prepare them for transfer of learning to larger contexts, the teacher will briefly

- Review the learning
- Monitor the level of success of all students
- Assign and integrate independent practice

Element 4: Independent Practice

Practice makes perfect. If the students practice errors, then they will err perfectly. It is essential that the teacher, in closing the lesson, determine whether the students have mastered the learning before sending them on down the road for independent practice. Once student mastery is confirmed, the teacher will assign tasks that cause students to practice what they have learned.

- Have students practice independently at home or in class
- Give feedback (delayed)
- Arrange independent practices several times over an extended period of days, weeks, or months

Structure of the Learning Climate

Keep in mind that a lesson need not include every direct instruction element. Therefore, the direct instruction model is better thought of as a series of questions to guide a teacher's decision making in planning for instruction. Among these questions are the following:

- How will students relate the new learning to what they already know or think they know?
- How will students obtain the necessary information?
- How will the teacher demonstrate or model the various key parts of the learning?
- As the lesson proceeds, what processes will the teacher use to determine the level of progressive understanding for *every* student in the class?
- What observed performance will substantiate that students are ready to move into independent practice?

The model is highly structured, held under the teacher's control throughout the entire lesson.

Teacher/Learner Interaction

The term *direct instruction* says it all. This process is directly controlled by the teacher. The flow, the progress, the decisions about whether or not to move

Figure 4.1   Direct Instruction Planning and Assessment Form

Pre-Planning

Teacher _____   Subject/Grade Level _____

Observer/Coach _____   Date _____

Overall Related Goal

Lesson Objective: (worded to guide the teacher in lesson development)

_____

_____

Instructional Models / Methods and Materials

Element 1: Orientation (Anticipatory Set)

Diagnosis and/or Relationship to Previous Learning	Statement of the Objective (worded for the students)	Directions for Students

Element 2: Teaching Input and Monitoring Understanding

Modeling Activities	Monitoring Activities	Guiding Practice Activities

Element 3: Closure

Final Monitoring	Restatement of the Objective	Observed Evidence of the Accomplished Learning

Element 4: Independent Practice

Immediate Independent Practice Activities	Delayed Independent Practice Activities

on to a subsequent point—all of these are directly determined by the teacher. The teacher carries out instruction, usually standing in front of the class and with much "teacher-talk," although that is not essential for direct instruction to occur. The teacher, using many techniques, involves the students, actively engaging them in their learning.

Outcomes

The outcomes of direct instruction are seen in instructional mastery of academic content and skills, in student motivation, and in self-pacing ability. They are also evident in enhanced self-esteem, nurtured through guided practice and the improvement experienced by the student.

Figure 4.1 provides a Direct Instruction Planning/Assessment Form, which may be useful for planning a direct instruction model lesson or for observing one and taking notes as to what occurs. An example of a direct instruction model lesson follows.

Sample Direct Instruction Lesson: Health Education

The following direct instruction lesson was developed by Karen Earl, following the format suggested by the Direct Instruction Planning and Assessment Form.

Overall Related Goal	Alcohol education
Lesson Objective (worded to guide the teacher in lesson development)	Students will evaluate case histories of alcoholics, determine which treatment option is best in each case, and defend their position.
Instructional Models / Methods and Materials	Six case histories and worksheets

Element 1: Anticipatory Set

Diagnosis and/or Relationship to Previous Learning	Statement of the Objective (worded for the students)	Directions for Students
"For the past five weeks you have been learning about various aspects of alcohol–its nature, the fact that it is a drug, its psychological and physiological effects. You know how it is used and abused as a 'socializing agent' in our culture."	"In this lesson, you will learn about treatments available to the alcoholic seeking recovery. You will find that they are many and varied."	"Listen carefully, for later you will be asked to list causes of alcoholism as they relate to the treatment mode you will have selected to defend."

Element 2: Input/Teaching/Presentation Activities

Modeling Activities	Monitoring Activities	Guided Practice Activities
Present the six different treatment options, their success rates, their costs, and elements of each treatment program.	Probing questions: Have you noticed this method in your reading? What success rate did the literature suggest for it? Can anyone assist [Susan] with this answer? Compare the claimed treatment successes of the various methods. What might cause a person to select one over the other? Compare methods (c) and (d). Which has the greatest success? Why do you suppose that is?	Read one of the case histories and discuss with class. Solicit opinions as to which treatment option this case could best use. Push students to defend their choice. Find students with opposing views and facilitate a brief debate. Hand out worksheets and instruct students to begin reading the case histories and responding to the worksheet. Teacher circulates around class, assisting individuals and monitoring the collective responses.

Element 3: Closure

Final Monitoring	Restatement of the Objective	Observed Evidence of the Accomplished Learning
Teacher facilitates a discussion of the worksheet, reviewing the six cases and the recommendations students made for treatment. Students defend their choices and are confronted by others with different choices.	"You have considered different treatment methods for alcoholism. What were they?" (Class reviews.)	"You have evaluated these six cases of alcoholism and recommended a treatment. There is one sure-fire thing to do about alcoholism so that treatments won't become necessary: *Don't use alcoholic beverages or other drugs.*"

Element 4: Independent Practice

Students are assigned to check in their community for alcoholism treatment facilities, interview the manager about treatments used, and write a "report of information" for class presentation next week.

MASTERY LEARNING

The core idea in *mastery learning* focuses on a system of major objectives in a unit or course, subdivided into smaller units with accompanying objectives, identified materials, and related tests for mastery, all sequenced toward cumulative mastery of the whole set. The work may be directed or self-paced. This view of learning assumes that learners acquire information best when it is broken down into component pieces and then systematically *laced together.* The teacher aggressively reinforces the previous learning and, as new pieces are added, continuously reviews the material to tie it together.

Teaching for mastery has its share of supporters and detractors. Properly implemented, mastery learning builds on the value of practice. Its proponents (Hunter, 1989) recognize that practice improves performance when it is designed and undertaken

- In small amounts that are rich in meaning
- In short, intense practice periods
- Frequently for new learning and regularly reviewed for older learning
- With specific, immediate feedback on results

Moreover, effective mastery learning calls for re-teaching with varied teaching strategies and media tailored to students' strengths and needs.

Unfortunately, some might argue that learning should be a mystery and a hurdle, made as challenging as possible if it is to be lasting and meaningful. Others seem to insist that learning must be facilitated with endless opportunities for practice until knowledge, skill, and application processes have been thoroughly mastered and internalized and the learner "gets it."

Certainly, repeated practice has its place. However, critics of mastery learning know that doing the same thing again and again leads not to true mastery, but rather to familiarity. They contend quite rightly that mere memorization has little value in itself.

Still, the mastery learning process, properly implemented, helps teachers make critical decisions as they plan for instruction. Mastery learning teachers select relevant motivational strategies. They devise ways to prepare students for learning, and they design individual meaning into the experiences they plan. These teachers create strategies for effective delivery of information. They decide how to address all learning modalities, styles, and intelligences. In advance, they identify means of demonstrating learning outcomes to students. They also figure out how to determine whether individual students are, in fact, mastering the content.

The key to mastery learning does not lie in memorization of identified bits of information. Rather, the much loftier goal is that students extend their thinking, raising it to levels of analysis, synthesis, and evaluation. Then, students will be able to transfer the concepts or outcomes they master to other domains of knowledge, skill, and understanding (Eisner, 1985; Hunter, 1989).

The strongest indicator of artistry and effectiveness in teaching is found in teaching for transfer. Very sophisticated teachers spend hours planning how to find and emphasize similarities across circumstances so that students can constructively transfer meaning from one subject to another. In mastery learning, such transfer must be the outcome, or we have merely induced simplistic memorization with no real learning.

ADVANCE ORGANIZER

The *advance organizer* is an especially useful tool to structure extended curriculum sequences or courses and to instruct students systematically in the key ideas of a field. It is based on pioneering work by David Ausubel (2000) to structure lesson delivery with the use of special or graphic organizers, leading to faster mastery and longer retention. With an advance organizer, teachers expect to increase the learners' grasp of factual information as it is linked to and explained by the key ideas. Models can be shaped in ways that greatly enhance skill and content mastery with an advance organizer (Katayama & Robinson, 2000). For example, in a lesson drawing together the events in American history of the past century, the teacher, Dan, attempted to lead students into identifying present-day results from decisions and actions that occurred in the post-Civil War United States. Students were presented with information they had covered in previous units and asked to summarize it according to these categories: Slavery and Political Aftermath; Reconstruction Politics in the South; and Unregulated Capitalism. As Dan presented information as well as source documents for later research, the students were guided into noting particular cause-effect relationships. Students suspected that these relationships could be traced forward to present-day moral lapses or social-moral conflicts. Thus, as shown in Figure 4.2, the advance organizer took the form of a chart into which students could enter their notes.

The Plan

An advance organizer can be formed into a special instructional model to serve as an introductory lesson in a unit. It might be more properly included in Chapter 5 of this book about information-processing models of teaching. It is

Figure 4.2 Sample Advance Organizer

Post-Civil War Social Influences	Notes
Historical Roots of Moral Decline	
Slavery and Political Aftermath	
Reconstruction Politics	
Unregulated Capitalism	

included here because of its frequent use, along with direct-instruction types of lessons, perhaps done as first in a series for a curriculum unit. This first lesson would be followed by components detailed in any number of the other instructional models. Joyce and Weil (2000) suggest that an advance organizer lesson would be constructed using three elements: (1) presentation of the advance organizer, (2) presentation of the material, and (3) strengthening of cognitive organization. These elements are outlined below.

Element 1: Presenting the Organizer

- The lesson objectives are made clear.
- The elements of the organizer are presented with samples and illustrations.
- The teacher probes and prompts students to discover their own previous understanding and information.

Element 2: Presenting the Information

- The instructionally relevant information is presented.
- The teacher deepens student attention to the information.
- The teacher makes the organized information explicit.
- The teacher discusses the integration of material by citing relationships among the data.

Element 3: Building Strong Cognition

- The teacher helps learners to deepen and apply their understanding about relationships among the pieces of information presented.
- The teacher encourages active learning and participation with the information.
- The teacher draws out of students the critical awareness necessary for deep understanding.
- The teacher relates the discussion to the lesson objectives and performance outcomes.

Structure of the Learning Climate

In this input-based, highly structured model, the teacher directly manages the flow of the lesson. Well-organized material is the critical support requirement of this model. The teacher continuously relates the information to the organizer as it is presented or encountered by the learners.

Teacher/Learner Interaction

The teacher responds to the students in several key ways:

- Continuously clarifying meaning
- Helping students to differentiate new information from existing understanding and integrating both

- Drawing student attention to relevancy of the information
- Promoting critical awareness

Outcomes

The instructional outcomes of the advance organizer model are conceptual structures, that is, the meaningful assimilation of information and ideas that students acquire. Nurturing outcomes are heightened interest in inquiry and more precise habits of thought.

The advance organizer as a model of teaching can provide a useful template for many different types of lessons wherein students must process large amounts of information to arrive at certain conclusions. The model can be a tool in the hands of students as they process large research problems or tasks and make personal decisions to guide their own learning.

PRACTICE THEORY

Another strategy, closely related to mastery learning, is practice theory. It involves six principles of effective practice (Joyce & Weil, 2000).

Six Principles of Effective Practice

1. The student should be shaped and moved through progressive levels of assistance, from lock-element guidance through guided practice to independent practice.

2. Length and frequency of practice sessions affect learning and retention curves; short, intense, highly motivated practice periods produce more learning than fewer but longer practice periods.

3. Monitoring the initial stage of practice is important so that students do not practice errors.

4. Students must approach high accuracy—say 90%—before they move to the next concept or sequenced lesson.

5. Distributed practice, that is, reinforcement spread out over time, heightens the level of retention for students.

6. In the beginning, the length of time between practice sessions must be short. Once the student has achieved the independent level of learning, however, practice is best distributed across longer periods.

Practice theory can be built into other models or used as a stand-alone model for mastery. More often than not, it is built into methods using components from other models. In many of the models discussed later in this book, we will see elements responding to one or more of the six principles listed above.

MEMORY MODEL

The *memory model,* another form of basic practice theory, is applicable to all curriculum areas in which material must be remembered. Although it has many uses in teacher-led "memory sessions," the memory model has widest application after students have mastered it and can use it independently as a learning tool.

The Plan

Planning to use the memory model requires four elements (Joyce & Weil, 2000): (1) attending to the material, (2) developing connections, (3) expanding sensory images, and (4) practicing recall. These are detailed as follows:

Element 1: Attending to the Material

- The students underline, listen, repeat, highlight, and so on.

Element 2: Developing Connections

- The students become thoroughly familiar with the information.
- Special mnemonic techniques are used, such as key word, association, and so on, to help in memorability.

Element 3: Explaining Sensory Images

- Students create exaggerated or ridiculous associations.

Element 4: Practicing Recall

- Students check one another in the recall of the information.

Structure of the Learning Climate

The instructional environment is cooperative in this model. The initiative should increasingly become the students' as they obtain control over the strategy and use it to memorize ideas, words, and formulas. All the customary devices of the curriculum areas can be brought into play—displays, object lessons, and audiovisuals such as computer projections, videos, digital display data, and so on—and are particularly helpful to promote association of information in memorable ways.

Teacher/Learner Interaction

The teacher helps students identify key items, pairs, and images—offering suggestions, but working from the students' frames of reference. The familiar elements must come primarily from the students' own storehouse of material and experience.

Outcomes

In the memory model, as in other behavioral models, we achieve instructional outcomes wherein students master facts and ideas. At the same time, they develop a system for memorizing and enhance their attending capabilities. The nurturing outcomes lead to a sense of intellectual power and creative attitudes and capacities.

THE MASTERY LECTURE METHOD

One useful method drawn from the behavioral models described above is called the *mastery lecture*. This method is created by blending the direct instruction model with segments from mastery learning, advance organizer, practice theory, and the memory model. Mastery lectures bring alive the age-old practices associated with lecturing by involving the learner in more than simply listening and writing notes. Rather, students are led from thinking about ideas and applying them to using them in practice.

The advance organizer helps students collect facts and ideas that ultimately lead to appropriate conclusions. Early theorists such as David Ausubel (2000) and Madeline Hunter (1976) proposed strategies like these to help students follow and process lecture content more easily and to help the teacher more effectively monitor student understanding and mastery as a lesson proceeds.

Teachers often use strategies of the mastery lecture when they want students to remember and understand facts or ideas that are important to a larger process. Such strategies involve

- Selecting a topic and identifying important information
- Designing an advance organizer
- Selecting questions to ask learners
- Presenting the advance organizer to students so that they can follow it throughout the lesson(s)
- Providing information through direct lecture, videos, books, tapes, or other media
- Asking questions throughout the presentation to monitor the learning
- Verifying the learning in a closure that revisits the purpose of the entire session

Introductory activities in the mastery lecture method are similar to the anticipatory set in the direct instruction model or to case orientation in other models. Element 2 activities represent the input, modeling, monitoring, and guided practice elements of the direct instruction model. Students are also asked to discuss in groups the information collected in the advance organizer. They need to draw interim conclusions, to practice remembering key understandings for later use, and to expand their notes in the organizer for later use in making conclusions. In Element 3, the teacher provides opportunities for practical application of the facts, concepts, or skills taught so that students can verify they have mastered the learning by the end of the session. Extended practice, closure, and independent practice from the direct instruction model are applied in this element. Also, the final elements of the advance organizer, memory, and mastery learning models are involved.

The Plan

The three elements of the mastery lecture method call for (1) introducing the topic, (2) providing information, and (3) making practical use of the information.

Element 1: Introducing the Topic

- Present an orientation using an advance organizer
- Probe students' initial understanding and relate the topic to that understanding
- Establish a focus on both the intended content and the processes of the lesson

Element 2: Providing Information

- Present information or guide students to information from various media sources
- Continuously connect, organize, and elaborate the content, assisting learners in relating the material to their personal lives
- Monitor student understanding and adjust teaching to ensure that all students are keeping pace
- Have students discuss the advance organizer and draw tentative conclusions

Element 3: Making Practical Use of the Information

- Provide opportunity to apply facts, concepts, or skills
- Provide extended practice
- Use closure activities
- Assign independent practice

Structure of the Learning Climate

In the mastery lecture method, the instructional environment is both directive and cooperative. The teacher presents but does not move forward until students have demonstrated mastery. All the customary devices used in the various curriculum areas can be brought into play. Pictures, concrete aids, films, and other audiovisual materials are especially useful because they enhance the sensory richness of the associations. Students work in groups to process the information provided to them.

Teacher/Learner Interaction

The teacher presents factual information, relates it to previous knowledge, helps students clarify and apply the new knowledge, and monitors their progress throughout the lesson. The teacher reinforces student learning by drawing attention to success.

Outcomes

Instructional outcomes are seen in student mastery of facts, ideas, or concepts and application to a practical level of understanding or skill. Nurturing outcomes can be observed in students' developing self-confidence as a result of their growing ability to remember factual information and make application to real problems. A sample lesson follows.

Sample Mastery Lecture Lesson: U.S. History, Civil War Roots of Modern Social Problems

Following is an application of the mastery lecture method to a lesson about the effects of the American Civil War on the development of our national culture.

Element 1: Introducing the Topic

- Show video clips from video disk on the outcomes of the Civil War
- Brainstorm the various social attitudes that class members have experienced that reflect attitudes discussed in the video
- Explain: "In this lesson and the next, we will consider the effects of the causes of the American Civil War on society and social relationships as we know them today. You will conclude with an essay on the subject."

Present the following advance organizer:

Advance Organizer: Civil War Roots of Modern Social Problems

- Causes of the Civil War
- Problems caused by the War
- Lingering race relations problems in the 21st century

Element 2: Providing Information

- One cause of the Civil War was the disagreement about whether people had the right to "own" other people.
- People of religious conviction were on both sides of the issue.

- Another related cause was economic. Slave labor was perceived to be essential for the Southern regions to compete with the Northern industrialized states.
- It was also essential for members of the upper class in the South to see themselves as "superior" to another entire race.
- Economic survival, a personal sense of worth and significance, and man's natural avarice, greed, and selfishness contributed to the war and its aftermath.
- But what of the industrialists in the North? They did not "own" people. But by keeping wages pitifully low, they ensured a large pool of labor, protected their profits, and fostered a class distinction that was just as devastating as the Southern system of slavery.
- Subtly keeping blacks undereducated, over many decades, meant that the pool of candidates eligible for successful leadership in business, government, and industry remained dominated by white males. Although there was no law making this occur, the dominant social attitudes suppressed blacks as effectively as did the Southern slave law.

Element 3: Making Practical Use of the Information

- By using texts, library resources, and handouts, have students list prominent blacks and whites after the Civil War and into the 20th century. How many can be found? What percentage of the overall population was black? What percentage of prominent individuals were black?
- Have students list the attitudes of whites toward blacks and vice versa as they exist today. Propose causes of these attitudes and give evidence.
- What efforts are being made to bring about racial harmony? Are they applied to racial groups other than blacks? Why or why not?

BEHAVIORAL MODELS FOR TEACHING AND LEARNING OUTCOMES

The models reviewed above are exciting and efficient to use. They are aimed at influencing student behaviors so that they *demonstrate* their levels of understanding of the material's instructional objectives. Some, like Joyce and Weil (2000), conclude that these models rely heavily on a behaviorist psychology of learning for their success. They tend to see the activities of the teacher as various levels of stimulus and reinforcement. But one need not be a committed psychological behaviorist to see successful uses for these models.

Phenomenologist thinkers (like me) tend to use applications of behaviorist and cognitionist strategies because the circumstances and the diagnosed need of the learner call for them both. Whether one uses a mastery lecture with an advance organizer, a memory or other practice theory model, a mastery learning approach or the time-tested direct instruction model, the student learning can be most effective. The trick, some say, is to vary the techniques according to student need from one day to the next.

Information-Processing Models

Guiding Questions

1. When is the *concept construction* type of model useful?

2. To which age groups might this model apply?

3. In what ways can the concept construction type of model serve as a "prewriting" activity in the writing process?

4. How can effective teachers use the *concept attainment* type of model to make learning fun?

5. How would the *synectics* model be useful to primary teachers? To middle grade teachers? To high school teachers?

6. Why is the synectics model so powerful a strategy?

In today's world, it is essential that students be taught to think—to process information in ways that lead them to findings, to conclusions, and to applications of new knowledge. The information-processing models embody a distinct point of view as to how people think and how to affect the ways they operate on information. The models represented in this chapter have been selected from both structured and unstructured categories: *concept construction, concept attainment,* and *synectics.*

CONCEPT CONSTRUCTION MODEL

The inductive thinking approach that we use to construct or create understanding of a conceptual idea is crucial to giving personal meaning to knowledge. Over the decades, creative teachers have used inductive teaching approaches for this purpose. Literature on teaching refers to these approaches as *concept development* (Gunter, Estes, & Schwab, 2003) or *concept formation* (Taba, 1967) models. The primary purpose of *concept construction* is to develop thinking capacity. In achieving this purpose, a teacher uses strategies that require students to ingest and process large quantities of information. Inductive processes include creative analysis of information, as well as convergent use of information to solve problems. The model closely resembles a prewriting strategy often referred to as "brainstorming."

This inductive thinking approach to learning can help if your students need to focus on

- Recalling and discriminating among main ideas
- Forming generalized concepts
- Recognizing relationships or patterns in the content
- Explaining reasoning clearly
- Citing proof or evidence

The model is best used in teacher-created methods that help students recall from prior knowledge, notice relationships, compare and contrast characteristics, explain how data are organized, and give evidence to support their organization of the data. It helps students to search out a concept by connecting and relating specific pieces of information. The teacher either presents specific data or calls on the students to brainstorm the ideas in a concept. Students must then place the generated data into groups or categories with descriptive labels. By relating the examples and labels, students develop an understanding of the concept.

The Plan

The four elements of the concept construction model are (1) familiarizing, (2) looking for relationships, (3) synthesizing information and consolidating insights, and (4) extended practice.

Element 1: Familiarizing

Have students

- Become familiar with the scope of the topic by listing relevant thoughts
- Expand the list

Element 2: Looking for Relationships

Have students

- Group the items listed in Element 1 in logically related clusters
- Give labels to clusters to help in categorizing the information
- Consider alternate relationships and regrouping the data
- Organize the clusters of data and determine relationships among clusters
- Collect the ideas that are inferred by the relationships discovered

Element 3: Synthesizing Information and Consolidating Insights

Have students

- Predict consequences and explain unfamiliar phenomena
- Verify their predictions and hypotheses
- Make generalizations and discuss concept applications

Element 4: Extended Practice

Have students

- Create new applications for the concept that has been developed; consider this a prewriting task for a writing assignment

Structure of the Learning Climate

The concept construction model has high to moderate structure. It is quite flexible in that teachers may or may not select to use any of the 11 elements outlined above in forming the most effective instructional method for a given situation. Concept construction is cooperative, but the teacher is the initiator and the controller of activities. The students need raw data to organize and analyze.

Teacher/Learner Interaction

The teacher uses eliciting questions that are matched to the students' level of cognitive activity and determines student readiness for the next element. Carried out in sequence, these elements reflect a natural thought process, one that most of us use in organizing information so that we can use it.

Outcomes

This model motivates students to become actively involved in their own learning and leads them to consider knowledge in a way that makes sense to them. It has both instructional and nurturing outcomes. The instructional outcomes include mastery of both the specific concept and the concept construction processes. Nurturing outcomes lead students to enhanced attention to logic, sensitivity to language, and awareness of the nature of knowledge.

Figure 5.1 is a planning sheet for creating a concept construction model lesson. Sample lesson plans are provided for you to review as you consider a particular lesson that you might like to teach with the concept construction model.

Figure 5.1 Concept Construction Planning Sheet

Objective _____

Element 1: Familiarizing

Orientation: Listing and Naming	Enumeration and Listing

Element 2: Looking for Relationships

Grouping	Categorizing and Labeling	Regrouping	Exploring	Drawing Inferences

Element 3: Synthesizing Information and Consolidating Insights

Predicting Consequences and Explaining Unfamiliar Phenomena	Verifying Predictions and Explanations

Making Generalizations

Element IV: Extended Practice

Creating New Applications

Sample Concept Construction Lesson: Musical Instruments

This sample lesson in concept construction was developed by Miriam Nishimoto Hamilton. Notice how she selected and adapted appropriate elements from the basic planning form.

Objective: The student will identify various musical instruments and classify them according to type: wind, brass, percussion, string.

Element 1: Familiarizing, Enumerating, and Listing

The teacher explains the procedure of concept construction to the students. She asks them to think of all kinds of musical instruments, listing them on paper. Then, the teacher has students call out their answers as she writes them randomly on the board.

Element 2: Looking for Relationships

Grouping	Categorizing and Labeling	Exploring Critical Relationships
Next, the teacher asks students which instruments seem to go together. According to students' suggested grouping, the teacher moves the arrangement of names on the board. Conflicts are left for continued discussion.	The teacher asks students to label the groups, making final decisions about the appropriate categories for all the instruments named. If students do not know the correct category name, they may make up a name for the time being.	Working in small groups, students are directed to explore reasons why the instruments are classified as they are. They are encouraged to identify the rationale for each categorization. With students back in the large group, the teacher guides the class through the procedure to determine correct labels.

Element 3: Synthesizing Information and Consolidating Insights

Predicting Consequences and Explaining Unfamiliar Phenomena	Verifying Predictions and Explanations
The teacher names an instrument that has not been discussed, and the students assign it to a category, defending the classification.	There are at least two ways to verify these predictions: One is through the teacher, and the second would be through a textbook or reference book. Perhaps a third would be to explore (hands-on) why the instrument should be in one category or another. For instance, the flute looks like a brass instrument but is really a woodwind. Students should be able to say it is a woodwind because of the direction of the airflow to produce the sound.

Element 4: Extended Practice

After the conclusion of the lesson, the teacher begins direct instruction about the concept of family among instruments, discussing what an orchestra is and how it is grouped. The teacher displays pictures of the instruments, or the actual instruments, and plays sample passages for each as well as samples of orchestrations.

Sample Concept Construction Lesson in Science: Newton's Laws of Motion

The next sample is a concept construction lesson in science. Again, note how the basic planning sheet is modified to suit the teacher's decisions about the lesson. This example was developed by Chuck Daniels.

Objective: Students will explain Newton's three laws of motion:

1. Objects in motion will maintain constant velocity unless acted on by an unbalanced force.

2. The more mass something has, the more force is required to accelerate it.

3. For every action, there is an equal and opposite reaction.

Element 1: Familiarizing

Set Up: Place a ball on a level ramp and ask why the ball does not move. Next, incline the ramp and ask why the ball rolls slowly down. Incline the ramp more and then ask why the ball accelerates.
Orientation: listing, naming, enumerating questions

1. What is happening here? What conclusions can you draw from what you have seen?

2. Why was the ball rolling down the ramp faster after the incline increased? What forces are at work in this example?

3. Will the ball continue to roll along the floor forever as it leaves the ramp? Why or why not?

4. Teacher holds out a 3 × 5 note card and a textbook. Teacher drops both at the same time. Book quickly falls to the floor as the card gently flutters down.

5. Why did the book fall faster? (Many students will say because it is bigger or has more mass.)

6. What would happen if there were no air resistance to get in the way of the card—how fast would it fall then? Why do you think that?

7. Next, the teacher places the note card flat on top of the book and asks if it will fall harder and faster than if the book were on top of the card?

Orientation: Listing and Naming	Enumeration and Listing
The teacher brings up the story of Galileo and the metal spheres he supposedly dropped from the top of the Leaning Tower of Pisa. The teacher reminds students that for over 2,000 years before Galileo, scholars believed that larger objects fell to the earth faster than lighter objects. The teacher has a methanol cannon on the desk. The cannon has a cork in one end and ignition apparatus on the other. As the cannon is fired, the cork goes to one direction as the cannon recoils in the opposite direction. The teacher asks for conclusions and observations.	The teacher leads a class discussion collecting the various observations and conclusions. A list is formed and the information grouped.

Element 2: Looking for Relationships

Categorizing and Labeling	Extension and Reorganization
The teacher facilitates a class discussion in which the listed observations are grouped and then the group clusters are entitled. Class members are asked to critique and defend their grouping and their titles.	The teacher has students reconsider groupings and suggests a few reorganizational changes. Other changes are elicited from students. A final observation chart is formed, explaining the physical activities illustrated in the opening.

Element 3: Generalizing

Ask students to summarize all the information into a single-sentence generalization about the concept.

Sample Concept Construction Lesson:
Literature and Drama, Critiquing Drama

This concept construction lesson plan in literature was developed for the high school level by Bill Cousins.

Objective: Students will evaluate several plays and movies and analyze various aspects of the dramatic content in order to appraise overall impact and performance.

Element 1: Familiarizing

Orientation: Listing and Naming	Enumeration and Listing
The teacher explains the concept of a brainstorming session. Students are then asked to recollect the recent story of *The Mayor of Casterbridge,* just finished in class, and to call out words and phrases associated with the tale.	The phrases are listed on the board as they are called out.

Element 2A: Looking for Relationships

Grouping	Categorizing and Labeling	Regrouping
The teacher asks students which story elements fit together and circles them in different colors. Any unrelated words or phrases are left aside for later discussion.	Students are asked to label the lists and categorize them under the main headings of character, plot, setting, and costume. Other group labels may be added if necessary.	The teacher suggests regrouping in other ways, for example, time scale, dramatic impact, winners and losers. Leftover items are discussed and placed into a list.

Element 2B: Looking for Relationships (continued)

Exploring Relationships	Drawing Inferences
In small cooperative groups, students are given a critic's theater review from a local newspaper. They are asked to examine the critic's play choices and identify the comments attributable to each category. Each group reports back to the class on one play, and the teacher leads discussion on the contrasting headings and their relationships.	The teacher draws inferences by comparing the newspaper review's groupings and those previously explored by the students from their reading book. The students are encouraged to examine any hierarchical dramatic traits that are common throughout the book.

Element 3: Synthesizing Information and Consolidating Insights

Predicting Consequences and Explaining Unfamiliar Phenomena	Verifying Predictions and Explanations
From the newspaper critic's choices, students are asked to rate the play on a scale of 1 to 10 and to defend their reasons. The teacher shows ratings on the board and illustrates the "for and against" comparison in each drama.	Using the ranking results, the teacher guides students in diagramming their thinking and rationale for the choices made. The teacher demonstrates why certain plays and movies are successes and failures while others are regarded as either good or bad. Students are encouraged to form conclusions based on essential dramatic components.

Element 4: Extended Practice

1. Homework assignment: Have students critically review a play or movie they have seen recently, justifying their remarks using the drama categorization techniques demonstrated in class.

2. Class activity: Show a video or arrange a class visit to a local play for classroom appraisal and discussion afterward.

3. Visiting speaker: Arrange for an actor to speak on his or her stage or film experiences.

Sample Concept Construction
Lesson: Science, the Microscope

This sample concept construction lesson was developed by Jason O'Neal in 1995. It develops concepts related to the microscope.

Objective: Students will identify various aspects of a microscope and classify according to: types, parts, magnification, and measurement.

Element 1: Familiarizing

Enumeration and Listing

The teacher explains the procedure of concept construction to the students and asks them to think of the various aspects of microscopes, listing them on the board. Possible examples: compound, electron microscope, arm, course adjustment, field size, "life size," objective lens, 4×, 10×, 40×, c = a • b/d.

Element 2: Looking for Relationships

Grouping

Next, the teacher asks students which aspects seem to go together. As students suggest a grouping, the teacher moves the arrangement of names on the board accordingly. Conflicts are left for continued discussion.

Categorizing and Labeling

The teacher asks students to label the groups, making final decisions about the appropriate categories for all named microscope aspects. If students do not know the correct category name, they may make up a name for the time being.

Exploring Critical Relationships

Working in small groups, students are directed to explore reasons why the aspects are classified as they are. They are encouraged to identify the rationale for each categorization. With students back in the large group, the teacher guides the class through the procedure to determine correct labels.

Grouping	Categorizing and Labeling	Exploring Critical Relationships
Possible groupings: *Group 1* compound electron stereoscope *Group 2* arm course adjustment ocular lens *Group 3* enlarging measure 10× *Group 4* field 1 = 2 field size c = a • b/d	Possible headings: Group 1 = types Group 2 = parts Group 3 = magnification Group 4 = measurement	Correct labels: 1 = types 2 = parts 3 = magnification 4 = measurement

Element 3: Synthesizing Information and Consolidating Insights

Predicting Consequences and Explaining Unfamiliar Phenomena

The teacher names an aspect that has not been discussed, and the students assign it to a category, defending the classification.

Verifying Predictions and Explanations

There are at least two ways to verify these categorizations: One is through the teacher, and another would be through a textbook or reference book. Perhaps another way would be to give students a handout. A fourth possibility is to have students reference a CD-ROM encyclopedia. For instance, the aspects *ocular* and *objective lens* could fit under the categories of parts and magnification. Students should be able to identify this because these aspects not only are parts of a microscope but also function on the microscope to magnify images.

Element 4: Extended Practice

At the conclusion of the lesson, the teacher begins direct instruction about the concept of mitosis. Following this instruction, students use different objectives on the microscope to identify the stages of mitosis.

CONCEPT ATTAINMENT

Human beings must communicate about literally millions of ideas. Language is limited in its ability to make these legions of communications. To identify just which ideas should be included in our school curricula, we turn to concepts. Concepts are expressions of big ideas from which we generalize permanent or semipermanent principles around which, in turn, we can organize our lives. Concepts include such things as love, hate, friendship, work, application, or any other number of terms that are compact expressions of very large, generalizable ideas encompassing much detail.

Concept attainment is the process of defining a "big idea" by attending to essential attributes, distinguishing them from associated attributes that are not essential to the meaning. The concept attainment model for teaching was developed by Marsha Weil (Joyce & Weil, 2000), based on the work of Jerome Bruner.

This model is designed to lead students to a concept by asking them to compare and contrast examples that contain the attributes of the concept with examples that do not contain such attributes. In various contexts, the model will

- Introduce an extended series of inquiries into important areas
- Augment ongoing inductive study
- Be interspersed throughout other inductive activities

Concept attainment consists of a class discussion, moderated by the teacher, seeking and listing attributes that can be used to distinguish exemplars from nonexemplars of focus ideas. It somewhat resembles the guessing game once popular as "20 questions"—except that there is no limit to the number of questions, and statements need not be phrased in question format.

The teacher begins by displaying positive and negative exemplars of the concept. Next, the teacher encourages students to hypothesize and cite possible exemplars, then confirms each example as either positive or negative. In the end, the teacher facilitates students' efforts to rationalize, analyze, and support their hypotheses as to what the "big idea" might be.

In preparing to teach this model, a teacher first selects the desired concept and writes a definition. Then, he or she identifies the essential attributes of the concept, as well as other associated attributes, or "anti-attributes," that are not essential.

The Plan

Weil's (Joyce & Weil, 2000) concept attainment model is planned in three elements: (1) presenting the data and identifying the concept, (2) testing student attainment of the concept, and (3) rehearsing the concept.

Element 1: Presenting the Data and Identifying the Concept

After presenting labeled examples, have students

- Consider examples of the concept against clarifying nonexamples
- Create a hypothesis and test it
- Create and report a definition through considering essential attributes of the concept

Element 2: Testing Student Attainment of the Concept

- The teacher asks students to distinguish further exemplars from nonexemplars, citing "yes" or "no" as they are presented
- The teacher confirms the hypothesis and repeats definitions created by students
- Students get to generate further positive exemplars

Element 3: Rehearsing the Concept

- Lead students to use the concept, applying it to an exercise designed to extend understanding
- Ask students to review the thought process used to attain the concept, assisting them to understand the process of relating attributes to one another until a concept is formed and understood as a whole

Structure of the Learning Climate

The model has moderate structure. The teacher controls the action, but free dialogue may develop within elements because student interaction is encouraged. Students gradually assume more initiative for inductive processes as they gain more familiarity with the model. Support consists of carefully selected and organized materials and data or pieces of information that serve as examples. As students become more sophisticated, they can share in making data units, just as in Element 2, they generate examples.

Teacher/Learner Interaction

The concept attainment model calls on the teacher to give guidance and support while also emphasizing the hypothetical nature of the discussion. This is done to help students balance one hypothesis against another, to focus attention on specific features of examples, and to assist students in discussing and evaluating their thinking strategies.

Outcomes

Instructionally, students come to understand the nature of concepts, their improved concept-building strategies, specific concepts, and inductive reasoning. They are also nurtured by enhanced awareness of alternative perspectives, tolerance of ambiguity coupled with appreciation of logic, and sensitivity to logical reasoning in communication.

Figure 5.2 presents a planning sheet for a concept attainment lesson plan, and a sample lesson follows here. After reviewing the sample lesson, try to create a concept attainment lesson to be delivered to your students and enhance their critical thinking abilities.

Figure 5.2 The Concept Attainment Planning Sheet

Objective _____

Planning

Concept	Concept Definition	Essential Characteristics

Element 1: Presenting the Data and Identifying the Concept

Positive Examples	Negative Examples	Possible Hypotheses

Element 2: Testing Student Attainment of the Concept

Unlabeled Examples

Element 3: Rehearsing the Concept

Application Exercise	Review

Sample Concept Attainment Lesson:
Intermediate French—The Imperfect Tense

The following sample concept attainment lesson was developed by Charlene DesRochers in 1996. The lesson teaches the concept of imperfect tense to students learning the French language.

Objective: Students will demonstrate an understanding of the imperfect verb tense in French and complete an exercise in which they will apply this understanding.

Planning

Concept	Concept Definition	Essential Characteristics
Imperfect tense L'imparfait	The passé composé is used to report what happened, and l'imparfait is used to report the circumstances or state of things in which incidents took place. Students attain this definition through lesson and examples.	Progressive actions in the past Habitual actions or conditions in the past

Element 1: Presenting the Data and Identifying the Concept

Positive and negative examples are illustrated in large letters on card stock in sentence form, then categorized on the board. The definitions are written on an overhead projector transparency. The attributes are written in the two columns on the board.

Positive Examples	Negative Examples	Possible Hypotheses
L'année dernière à cette date, j'étais en Egypt. Nous étions dans le voisinage au moment de l'accident.	Souvenez-vous du terrible accident qui a eu lieu sur le Nil? Qu'est-ce qui est arrivé, exactement?	Students are asked to compare attributes in Element 1 (positive and negative examples), then generate and test hypotheses as to what this idea is.
C'était un très vieux bateau. "Helene, vous étiez avec moi quand le bateau a peine venait de quitter la rive . . .	Le jour de l'accident, ils ont embarqué plus de cent cinquante personnes dans le vieux bateau. . . . lorsque l'eau a commencé a entrer à l'intérieur."	

In Element 2, students are asked to hypothesize still more and to provide a definition of their preferred term.

Positive Examples	Negative Examples	Possible Hypotheses
Le bateau était si près du bord . . . Naturellement, plus ils tiraient sur les cordes, plus le bateau s'inclinait.	. . . que le capitaine a lancé des cordes à des gens sur la rive du fleuve. Il a fini par chavirer.	Students attain the idea of the imperfect tense as a past tense requiring the verb endings *ais, ais, ait, iez, ions, aient*. Students distinguish imperfect from past tense.

Element 2: Testing Student Attainment of the Concept

Unlabeled Examples

Students identify the Element 2 examples and then provide many more of their own. They remain faithful to the developing idea of the "imperfect tense" for verbs describing progressive continuous action in the past, or verbs describing habitual actions or the state of being in the past. Students can separate the imperfect from the passé composé, which describes or reports actions that happened and were completed in the past without a continuous progression. Students narrow and eliminate all inappropriate statements of the concept, leaving the correct ones.

Element 3: Rehearsing the Concept

Application Exercise	Review
Students apply the concept to an exercise designed to extend understanding. That exercise includes describing an event that happened in the past along with describing the state of things at the time the event occurred.	Students review the thought process (categorizing, forming and relating attributes, forming hypotheses, and developing a definition), all with teacher guidance, but not direction.

Sample Concept Attainment
Lesson: Language—Action Verbs

The next sample concept attainment lesson, developed by Karen Smithe, addresses the part of speech we call *verbs*. Again, the format follows the three elements of the model, adapted to the teaching situation.

Previous Learning: Introduction to language idea of verbs, accomplished in previous grades

Lesson Time: approximately 20 minutes

Relationship of Objective to Other Class Activity: This objective is related to a concurrent literature story, "Zoo," by Edward Hoch. The objective is an introduction to the "vivid verbs" language concept in conjunction with the story.

Objective: Students will identify and define "vivid verbs," naming essential attributes of categorized positive examples.

Planning

Concept	Concept Definition	Essential Characteristics
Vivid verb	The word in a sentence that expresses an act or occurrence	Action words; words that describe doing something; words that say you did something; words that describe somebody doing something; and so on.

Element 1: Presenting the Data and Identifying the Concept

Positive and negative examples are illustrated in large letters on card stock, then categorized on easel paper. The definitions are written on an overhead projector transparency. The attributes are written in the two columns on the easel paper.

Positive Examples	Negative Examples	Possible Hypotheses
→ jumped → talked → shouted → watched	→ spaceship → creatures → zoo → Professor Hugo	In Element 1, students are asked to compare attributes in positive and negative examples, then generate and test hypotheses as to what this idea is.
→ stopped → planned	→ earth → constantly	In Element 2, the students are asked to hypothesize still more and provide a definition of their preferred term.

Students will attain the idea of "vivid verbs" as action words.

Element 2: Testing Student Attainment of Concept

Students will identify the Element 2 examples and then provide many more of their own, keeping fidelity to the developing idea of "action words." Students will narrow and eliminate all inappropriate statements of the concept, leaving the correct ones.

Element 3: Rehearsing the Concept

Application Exercise	Review
Students will apply the concept to an exercise designed to extend understanding.	Students will review the thought process (categorizing, forming, and relating attributes, forming hypotheses, and developing a definition), all with teacher guidance, but not direction.

Sample Concept Attainment Lesson: Literature—Theme

The following sample concept attainment lesson was developed by Regina Choo to address the literary quality we call theme. Developed for a secondary classroom, the lesson applies the concept attainment model to analyze the novel To Kill a Mockingbird.

Objective: Students will demonstrate understanding of the literary element of theme, first as related to the novel *To Kill a Mockingbird,* by proposing and discussing essential attributes of categorized examples. Students will then write their own definition for *theme* and extend their understanding of this concept by formulating statements of theme for five recently read works of fiction.

Planning

Concept	Concept Definition	Essential Characteristics
Theme	The central point or message the writer is trying to communicate through a piece of literature	Statement of the author's purpose and intent in writing the literature; arises from an understanding of the other elements of the literature (e.g., character, plot, conflict); must be a complete thought stated in the form of one or more sentences

Element 1: Presenting Data and Identifying the Concept

Positive Examples	Negative Examples	Possible Hypotheses
1. To judge and understand a person, you must try to see things from his or her perspective. 2. White and black people are inherently equal. 3. It is more valiant to fight with one's head than one's fists. 4. It is a sin to harm an innocent, defenseless creature (such as a mockingbird). 5. The individuality of each human being should be tolerated and respected.	1. Atticus Finch 2. Prejudice and its effect on the judicial process 3. Scout matures with the help of her dad. 4. Maycomb, Alabama, during the Depression 5. The mockingbird symbolizes both Tom Robinson and Boo Radley. 6. Scout tries to control her temper because it is one of the few things Atticus has ever asked of her.	The students are asked to propose new examples that they believe represent the concept. The teacher classifies each student-generated example as either positive or negative. Based on a comparison of the positive and negative examples, students formulate a list of hypotheses that characterize or define the concept.

Positive Examples	Negative Examples	Possible Hypotheses
6. Dignity and respect are earned by your character and your actions, not money or the color of your skin.		As more positive and negative examples are identified and analyzed, students reflect on the list of possible hypotheses. They eliminate those that are no longer plausible, thus narrowing and refining the list.

Element 2: Testing Student Attainment of Concept

Unlabeled Examples

The teacher provides further examples:

People's privacy should be respected. (+)

Real courage is knowing you will lose, but continuing to fight the battle. (+)

Scout is pressured by her aunt to be more ladylike. (−)

Being a lady is not what you wear, but how you act. (+)

Miss Caroline is wrong to be upset with Scout's reading ability. (−)

Scout matures through her experiences at the trial. (−)

Students are asked to predict whether each example is positive or negative. This process continues with additional student-generated examples. Students narrow and eliminate all inappropriate statements of the concept from the list of hypotheses until only the essential characteristics remain. Using this list and class discussion of the multifaceted meaning of *theme* (focusing on how all previous learned elements of literature are integrated in discovering the theme[s] of a work), students write individual definitions of the concept.

Element 3: Rehearsing the Concept

Application Exercise

Students are given a list of five recently read pieces of fiction. For each piece of literature, students study the interactions of characters, conflicts, subject, and plot in an attempt to identify the author's purpose for writing the piece. Students write a possible statement of theme for each piece. In small groups, students read one of their statements of theme and explain the process they have used to reach that understanding of the theme of the particular work.

SYNECTICS

William Gordon (1961) has developed an approach to teaching that enhances learner creativity. The processes are developed from views of creative learning. He suggests that by bringing the creative process to the conscious level and by developing explicit aids to it, we can directly increase the creative abilities of learners. Use of metaphors and analogies has long been known to open avenues of creative thought. In business and industry, problem solvers frequently use this technique to open new vistas and to help workers see a problem from a whole new perspective.

In the synectics approach, students first are presented with a *concept* and an *analogue* to which it is compared. They are asked to consider how the concept might be explained in terms similar to its analogue. Next, they think in the *personage* of both the *concept* and its *analogue*. This element is followed by comparing the concept and analogue to discover how they are dissimilar instead.

The process gives students new and "outside the box" perspectives about the concepts they are studying. It is important that teachers use analogues or analogies with which students are quite familiar. In making comparisons of a concept under study with an analogous idea that they know well, they can draw new insights about the object of study. Two strategies, both adapted from Gordon (1977), are suggested as having a particularly powerful impact on lesson design.

The Plan: Strategy 1

Element 1: Identification of What Is

- Have students describe the situation as they see it

Element 2: Create a Representative Analogy

- Ask students to suggest analogies that represent the original concept
- Students discuss the analogy and investigate all the ways it represents the original concept

Element 3: Impersonating the Analogy

- Students will adopt the persona of the analogy, examining thoughts and feelings

Element 4: Students Invent New Analogy

- Have students suggest a different analogy and explain how it represents the original concept

Element 5: Refocus on the Lesson Concept

- Teacher leads learners to reconsider the original lesson concept and examine it in light of the discoveries produced by the analogous thinking

The Plan: Strategy 2

A second strategy suggests the following sequence of activities.

Element 1: Teacher Suggests Analogy

- The teacher presents an idea, question, or concept to students and suggests its complexity.
- The teacher then suggests a particular analogy to explain or illustrate the original concept.
- The teacher then leads the class in discussing the related ideas to the analogy as illustrative of the original concept.

Element 2: Second Analogy

- The teacher will then suggest another analogous idea, this time asking students to explain how the concept under examination might be considered to be similar to the familiar analog.

Element 3: Impersonating the Analogy

- The teacher has students impersonate or "become" both the analogue and the concept. During a facilitated discussion, they speak as if the concept or the analogue were speaking.

Element 4: Contrasting the Analog With the Concept

The teacher

- Encourages students to recognize the points where the concept and the analog are similar and different
- Asks the students to explain and defend points where the analog does not fit with the concept
- Asks students to review the original concept and consider new implications about it drawn from the analogous thinking

Element 5: Inventing a New Analogy

In this strategy, the teacher also invites students to consider one final analogy to represent the idea under study and explain why it holds meaning for them as representative of that idea.

Structure of the Learning Climate

Teachers bring a moderate level of structure to this model. They initiate the sequence and then guide students in using the analogous process. Students have freedom in open-ended discussions to express and think.

Teacher/Learner Interaction

By noting the extent to which students relate to systematic patterns of thought, teachers attempt to induce psychological states that will generate creative responses. The nonrational is used; reluctant students are encouraged to indulge in irrelevance, fantasy, and symbolism, thus breaking out of established patterns of thinking.

Outcomes

The instructional outcomes in synectics lead to an enhanced creative capacity within subject domains. Nurturing outcomes include achievement in subject domains along with group cohesion and productivity.

Synectics, used within a diverse, integrated, thematic curriculum, is suitable for writing creatively, exploring social problems, solving problems, creating a design or a new product idea, or broadening individual or group perspective on a concept. Below is a sample synectics lesson. After reading it, think through the processes and create a synectics lesson for one of your classes.

Sample Synectics Lesson: U.S. History—Causes of the Civil War

The sample synectics lesson below addresses the start of the Civil War in the elements outlined above from Strategy 2.

Objective: Students will write a paragraph about the major causes of the Civil War beyond the idea that it was all about preventing slavery.

Element 1

The teacher presents newspaper stories about the economic crisis in the northern states in the mid 1800s. He explains that, although there were many who were against the policy of slavery, the major decision makers in the northern states were industrialists who had to compete against the newly formed Confederate economy. The Confederate economy was based on the relatively low-cost labor of slaves. It is suggested that the main reason industrialists were willing to invest millions of dollars into forcing a stop to slavery was more about ending this source of free labor among business competitors in the southern states. In that light, the teacher says that the cause of the Civil War was like two children arguing over who gets a fair share of the sweets. She illustrates this analogy with stories about children squabbling over their fair share.

Element 2

Next, the teacher suggests another direct analogy for the causes of the Civil War. She says that the start of the war is like a *sickness.* Only this time, she is asking students to explain how the concept—causes of the Civil War—might be considered to be similar to the familiar analogue—an illness. As the students pose ideas, the teacher prompts and probes the ideas to enrich the meaning and the relationships.

Element 3

The teacher then asks the students to impersonate or "become" both the analogue and then the concept. They speak as if the concept or the analogue were speaking. First, they speak as a voice that causes an illness in the body. Then, they describe their feelings as if they were a voice that was pushing for warfare among the states.

Element 4

In this stage, the teacher asks students to identify and explain the points of similarity between the causes of an illness and the causes of the Civil War. This is then followed with a prompted discussion about how the causes of an illness are *not* like the causes of the Civil War. The latter may have been decisions of the will, whereas the former may have been beyond the control of the person's body. She has students explain where the analogy does not fit.

She then asks students to explore the original topic again, on its own terms, list other possible causes of the Civil War, and explain them.

Element 5

The teacher then guides students as they create their own direct analogies and explore the similarities and differences between their concepts and their analogues in terms of the Civil War. They conclude by writing as their homework assignment an essay of four paragraphs (first draft) about the causes of the Civil War.

Sample Synectics Lesson: Music

This lesson by Kathi Williams illustrates the use of the synectics strategy with middle grade music students.

Objective: Students will create a four-measure melodic musical composition using at least six different musical symbols

Element 1: Describing the Topic

The teacher tells a story of a young boy who needs to find a new home. The boy searches on one street where all the people sing and talk very high (the treble clef). As the teacher is telling the story, she draws the treble and bass clefs and staff, pointing to where the young boy might be looking for a new home.

After the young boy decides he does not want to live in a place where he must speak and sing either high or low all the time, he decides he wants to live right in the middle. The teacher draws middle C between the two staves.

The teacher also explains that as the notes go up on the staves, the pitch goes up. She then demonstrates by writing on the board that the musical notes are assigned an alphabet letter, A through G.

Element 2: Creating Another Analogy

The teacher suggests that written music is like a road map. There are many symbols that tell us where to go next, how fast we can go, and when to stop. Written music represents musical sound in motion. The teacher asks the students to look in their music textbooks for music map symbols. The class discusses what the symbols mean in music and what they each would represent in a similar situation on a road map.

Element 3: Describing Personal Analogies

The teacher asks students to select one of the musical symbols and explain to the class what it would be like to be that symbol. What are you telling people to do? What will happen if everyone does not follow the rules you require as a music symbol?

Element 4: Comparing Analogies

The students are asked to discuss the general similarities between a road map and a written composition. The teacher then asks students to call out several road map symbols (e.g., speed limit, bridge, legend, etc.) and the corresponding music symbols. She lists them on the board.

Element 5: Explaining the Differences

The teacher asks students to discuss how the analogy does not fit with music. Symbols are not the same, cars are not used, you don't actually move your body from one place to another, and so on.

Element 6: Exploration

The teacher asks students to write a four-measure melodic phrase incorporating at least six music symbols listed on the board. Grading is based on the proper use of the symbols and on the musicality of the melodic phrase chosen.

Element 7: Generating Another Analogy

The teacher asks students to get with another person and develop another analogy for written music. The students then share their original ideas with the rest of the class.

Sample Synectics Lesson:
Lifelong Ethical Decisions for Athletes

Jon Speir asks senior athletes to consider decisions that many young-but-proficient athletes must face as they proceed through their college athletic careers. The reality is that many young athletes can help teams win games, but their availability is limited by potential injuries during college portions of their careers. As a result, professional athletic teams recruit mid-college athletes because they work cheaper. Accordingly, they do not finish college and are not prepared for a career outside of athletics, should they become incapacitated in the sport due to injury. Jon urges young aspiring athletic stars to seriously consider their options and the options that a truly effective college education can give them.

Objective: Students will write a paragraph about the trend of athletes who leave their universities prior to graduation to turn professional, evaluating the ethics and the repercussions involved.

Element 1: Describing the Topic

The teacher asks students to give motives for staying in school versus leaving a free education and trying to be a professional athlete. He asks them to give actual scenarios of individuals who decided to finish their college career along with those individuals who decided to leave to play professionally. Then, he makes two columns on the board labeled "*Stay in School*" and "*Go for the Pros!*" He lists the responses on the board.

Element 2: Creating Direct Analogies

The teacher suggests an analogy for both circumstances. He offers a story about two country mice. Both mice wanted to work in the big city at a cheese plant. However, this was a very difficult position to acquire because it was very popular. In fact, mice must be chosen to go to a special school in order to hope to be even a security guard at these cheese plants. Yet, if they are never able to work as a cheese maker, they can always use the free education they received and make Velveeta.

Both mice were chosen to go to the special school in hopes of becoming cheese makers. But one of the mice was so efficient in school that he was given the opportunity to work at the local cheese plant after his second year. He chose to do so and made a lot of cheese. At the same time, the other mouse was still working on his free education. He was learning about many subjects and learned that he could be skilled at many jobs after college.

Five years later, the mouse with the completed education began his career as a cheese maker. He was happy. The mouse who had left school early was not so fortunate. Although he was a superstar for a year and earned a position on the board of cheese makers, something terrible happened to him. He lost his paw in the Swiss cheese hole-puncher. The company could not keep him because his position was so important, and without both paws, he could not fulfill its requirements. And, without an education, he could not do any other type of work for the company. He returned to the farm rejected and wondering about his life choices.

The teacher asks the class to select one of the mice and discuss the wisdom of the choices he made.

Element 3: Describing Personal Analogies

The teacher next asks students to imagine themselves in the place of a college athlete. What would they do if they were offered a position on a professional football team? Would they give up their free education and "go for it"? Would they fulfill the commitment they made with the university to play 5 years and get their free education? The students must decide one of the two options and explain why. Next, the teacher asks the students to speak as *the Sports Career* enticing the athlete to leave school and come play. Then, they are asked to speak as the *Free Education* they could be getting by completing their university commitment before turning professional.

Element 4: Creating a New Direct Analogy

The teacher then asks students to work in pairs and create a different analogy or story that illustrates the issues involved in professional athletics recruiting away college athletes prior to their completion of school. The pairs will share their analogy or allegory with the class.

Element 5: Reexamining the Original Question

The teacher asks students to review the original question: whether it is best for college athletes to complete their schooling before turning professional or to become professional while they are in the midst of college. He asks them to present a scenario wherein they decide to play a sport but become permanently injured. How would it come out? Next, students present a scenario wherein they completed education, began to play a sport, and were permanently injured. What options exist then?

The teacher then engages the class members in a Socratic dialogue about each pair of scenarios and pushes them to make a defensible decision for their own sports career plans.

6

Teaching Through Inquiry

Guiding Questions

1. What is *inquiry* teaching, and what makes it such an effective teaching approach?

2. How would you use *inquiry training* as a teaching model and why?

3. Social science inquiry is quite common in higher levels of education; what makes it so useful?

4. Scientific inquiry has been made famous in the long-taught *scientific method*, but why?

5. What are some excellent ways to structure questioning strategies for use with inquiry lessons?

6. What is most important to you regarding the way questions are used to enhance student learning outcomes?

Inquiry is an instructional process involving the asking and answering of questions. Teachers have always used questions as a tool to guide learners to new understanding, to truth, and to skill application. This chapter focuses mainly on questioning strategies. The probing and prompting techniques presented here are applicable in almost all models, but especially in inquiry models. Teachers may weave together interesting and challenging strings of questions for students to ponder as they discover knowledge and apply skills. An inquiry model may place responsibility for questioning on either the teacher or the learner. In a sense, all teaching could be said to involve inquiry. However, in models that use inquiry as the key to lesson design, the process is more intentional and purposeful. Below are discussions of the *inquiry training, scientific inquiry, Socratic inquiry,* and *social science inquiry* models.

INQUIRY TRAINING

The inquiry training model calls on students to obtain information by asking questions that are answered with yes or no. The construction of puzzling instructional situations is critical to this methodology because it transforms curriculum content into problems to be explored. Teachers present students with a problem statement and collections of facts, or they lead students in collecting and constructing a database relating to the problem statement. The model, described by Bruce Joyce and Marsha Weil (2000), is found with variations in many books about teaching strategies.

This model—sometimes referred to as a "guess what I know" lesson—may be criticized as being less than efficient at teaching information. This is not the methodology to use when the goal is mastery of specific information or facts. Inquiry learning teaches thinking and problem solving.

The Plan

Joyce and Weil (2000) suggested that planning occurs in five elements: (1) confronting the problem, (2) gathering and verifying data, (3) gathering data from experimentation, (4) organizing and formulating an explanation, and (5) analyzing the inquiry process. This process is outlined below.

Element 1: Confronting the Problem

The teacher

- Introduces the process of questioning and examining curiosities and items provoking those curiosities
- Presents information that initiates a questioning process or experimentation

Element 2: Gathering and Verifying Data

The teacher has students

- Recognize the facts about the curiosity or focus
- Check to be sure that the phenomenon is real and repeats itself

Element 3: Gathering Data From Experimentation

The teacher leads students to

- Find variables and check them individually for impact on the curiosity
- Create hypotheses that explain their observations.

Element 4: Organizing and Formulating an Explanation

The teacher supports students as they prepare explanations of the phenomenon or curiosity and probes them as they seek to clarify it.

Element 5: Analyzing the Inquiry Process

The teacher leads students to review their procedures and check to see that there were no other variables introduced or inconsistencies in the rounds of experimentation.

Structure of the Learning Climate

The teacher controls the interaction and prescribes the inquiry procedures. However, the norms of inquiry call for cooperation, intellectual freedom, and equality. Interaction among students should be encouraged, and the teacher and students also interact as mutual investigators. The teacher plays the role of *guide* as the students make inquiry about the problem.

Teacher/Learner Interaction

Using inquiry training, the teacher

- Ensures that questions are phrased so they can be answered with yes or no and that their substance does not require the teacher to do the inquiry
- Asks students to rephrase invalid questions
- Points out nonvalidated points, for example, "We have not established that this is liquid"
- Uses the language of the inquiry process, for instance, identifies student questions as theories and invites testing of the theory
- Tries not to evaluate student theories so as to provide a free intellectual environment
- Presses students to make clearer statements of theories and to support their generalizations
- Encourages interaction among students

Outcomes

Instructional outcomes of inquiry training enhance scientific process skills and strategies for creative inquiry. Nurturing outcomes are seen in the developing spirit of creativity, greater independence or autonomy in learning, tolerance for ambiguity, and recognition of the tentative nature of knowledge.

SCIENTIFIC INQUIRY

Scientific inquiry is an appropriate model to use in science classes or integrated courses involving science information. The essence of this approach is teaching students to process information using techniques similar to those of research biologists: identifying problems and using a particular method to arrive at solutions. This model may be generally applied to social science instruction as well, teaching students to assess human behavior. Joyce, Weil, and Showers (1991, 1995) suggested a five-element plan: (1) focus, (2) problem analysis, (3) hypothesizing, (4) experimentation, and (5) conclusions.

The Plan

Element 1: Focus

The teacher will first suggest an area of inquiry.

Element 2: Problem Analysis

After some discussion, the teacher leads the students in identifying the issue by asking questions (as in inquiry training).

Element 3: Hypothesizing

If students do not do so quickly, the teacher motivates them to form hypotheses or ideas explaining their observations.

Element 4: Experimentation

The teacher facilitates the students' attempts to structure and conduct experiments about their area of inquiry.

Element 5: Conclusions

The students next draw conclusions. They develop their ideas into various forms of *report of findings*. They may speculate about future investigations that are necessary because of what they have discovered.

Structure of the Learning Climate

This model requires the teacher to develop a learning climate in which cooperation and enthusiasm abound. Students need to be bold in their inquiry and humble in their outcome, willing to accept results without disappointment. The areas of potential inquiry or problems to explore should be realistic, meaningful, and, by the way, plentiful.

Teacher/Learner Interaction

As the learners investigate, the teacher nurtures their questioning of the subject and their reflection on the investigation as it unfolds. As students recognize certain facts, they must be encouraged to move forward toward conclusions about questions rather than the mere identification of those facts.

Outcomes

The instruction results in mastering a process of research commonly used in the biological and physical sciences. Nurturing outcomes come in the forms of confidence with scientific knowledge and commitment to scientific inquiry. Students are able to remain open-minded as they consider various alternative explanations and demonstrate their potential reliability.

SOCRATIC INQUIRY

The Socratic inquiry model of teaching is designed to bring about higher order thought in considering difficult issues. This model may not be appropriate for young children. However, a middle or high school unit or course in which public issues drive major objectives can be totally designed around Socratic inquiry. This process differs from the other inquiry models in that the teacher poses most of the questions.

The Socratic questioning process, however, can be integrated into lessons designed for any grade level to create blended model methods that best meet the needs of particular teachers for particular students and content. Therefore, this model is useful even in the quiver of the primary teacher. The model is based on the work of Oliver and Shaver (1971). It gives learners a conception of society in which people differ in their views and priorities and in which social values legitimately conflict with one another. Three areas of competency are necessary, according to Bruce Joyce (Joyce & Weil, 2000):

- A values framework
- A set of clarification skills
- Knowledge of contemporary political and public issues

Socratic inquiry as a teaching model is built on Socratic dialogue, in which a student takes a position and the teacher challenges that position with questions. Because most arguments center on definitions, values, or facts, participants must explore all three as they investigate each other's positions and assess the strengths and weaknesses of alternative stances.

A basic problem in discussions of social issues is ambiguous or confusing use of words. We must find common meaning in our discussions. Therefore, to bring about mutual and concomitant understanding, a teacher must insist on probing all terms and concepts that students present.

The Plan

This model (Joyce & Weil, 2000) consists of six elements of exploration by students, guided by their teacher: (1) orienting to the case; (2) identifying the issues; (3) taking positions; (4) exploring the stances underlying the positions; (5) refining and qualifying positions; and (6) testing assumptions about facts, definitions, and consequences. The six elements are grouped into two procedures: investigation and analysis (Elements 1 through 3) and argumentation (Elements 4 through 6). Elements 1 through 4 could take up an entire class period, followed by Element 5 as individual or group work and Element 6 in a follow-up class or as an end-of-unit activity.

Investigation and Analysis

Element 1: Orienting to the Case

The teacher presents the concern and introduces facts and background information, drawing on written, video, or formal investigative sources.

Element 2: Identifying the Issues

The second element is a study process in which students synthesize facts into an issue, characterize related values, and identify conflicts between values. The teacher begins to guide students to

- Synthesize facts into one or more public policy issues
- Select one policy issue for discussion
- Identify values and value conflicts
- Recognize underlying factual and definitional questions

Element 3: Taking Positions

In Element 3, students are encouraged to speak on an issue in seminar or panel format. Students are led to

- Articulate a position
- State the basis of their position in terms of the social value or consequences of the decision

Argumentation

Element 4: Exploring the Stances Underlying the Positions

Moving on to argumentation, the teacher shifts into a confrontational style, probing student positions. In doing this, a teacher may use any of four patterns of argumentation:

- Establish the point at which a value is violated (factual)
- Prove the desirable or undesirable consequences of a position (factual)
- Clarify the value conflict with analogies
- Set priorities, assert priority of one value over another, and demonstrate lack of gross violation of the second value

Element 5: Refining and Qualifying Positions

Element 5 involves refinement and qualification of positions. This often naturally flows out of the Element 4 dialogues, although occasionally, the teacher must prompt students to restate positions. Reasoning and values are clarified. The students should

- State their position and reasons for the position
- Examine a number of similar situations
- Qualify the position

Element 6: Testing Assumptions
About Facts, Definitions, and Consequences

The teacher guides students to check their assumptions and to see whether their positions remain consistent under very extreme conditions. Have the students

- Identify factual assumptions and determine relevancy
- Determine the predicted consequences and examine factual validity for each

Socratic inquiry is not a lesson model suited to a single class period but, rather, typically requires several days of class activity for the first three elements and at least another couple of hours to complete Elements 4 through 6.

Structure of the Learning Climate

The model has either a moderate or a high level of structure. The teacher will begin and influence the flow of discussion, but he or she also facilitates an open and receptive climate in pursuit of highest order thinking. The documentation and resources needed must be clearly focused on the problem.

Teacher/Learner Interaction

The teacher, using the following strategies, can produce an open and interactive climate by

- Avoiding direct evaluation of students' opinions
- Seeing that issues are thoroughly explored
- Probing the substance of students' thinking through questioning relevance consistency, specificity, generality, definitional clarity, and continuity

If the teacher is to maintain a dialogical style, he or she will regularly

- Use confrontational dialogue
- Question students' assumptions
- Use specific instances (analogies) to contradict more general statements
- Take care not to advocate a particular stand

Outcomes

Instructional outcomes give students a framework for analyzing social issues, the ability to assume the role of "the other," and competence in social dialogue. Nurturing outcomes lead to an enhanced capacity for social involvement, desire for social action, knowledge of facts related to social problems, and empathy and awareness relating to cultural pluralism.

Socratic inquiry provides a framework for creating contemporary course content involving public affairs. Also, it is a process for dealing with conflict in the domain of public issues. It is tailored to older students and must be considerably modified at the junior high and middle school level.

Socratic questioning can be considered a process separate from the Socratic inquiry model; in Socratic questioning, a teacher uses only the fourth and fifth elements. The teacher asks open-ended questions, leading students into exploration of topics that they may have actively prepared or into review of material that they had gradually mastered over time. In this alternative form, the model is also referred to as the *class discussion model* (Gunter, Estes, & Schwab, 1995).

Teachers must permit time for Socratic inquiry to run its course. Examination of a single case should be allowed to continue for several days. This gives students the chance to acquire information, reflect on ideas, and develop confidence and courage of position. It would be counterproductive to set up short, one-time debates over complex issues. Formal instructional sessions teaching students directly about analytic and argumentative techniques may be useful, but these should be introduced naturally and slowly. Socratic questioning or classroom discussion models, on the other hand, may easily be used for either partial or whole class periods.

For years, social studies courses have been successfully organized around the study of cases. This model increases the vigor and intensity of students as they process the information and cast about for solutions to problems.

Sample Socratic Inquiry Lesson: U.S. History—Immigration to the United States

Working with his high school history students, Mark Gotts applied the Socratic inquiry model to a study of immigration to the United States.

Objective: Students will investigate immigration trends and history and present supported views regarding U.S. immigration policy.

Investigation and Analysis

Element 1: Orienting to the Case

(First class) Students are presented with data drawn from recent immigration statistics. These data include figures regarding legal and illegal immigration by country of origin. Also included are occupations of the immigrants. This information is to be compared with trends in immigration to the United States over the past century. The stories of some immigrants who have influenced our country are presented (e.g., Alexander Graham Bell and Gloria Estefan).

Element 2: Identifying the Issues

(Second class) Students are guided to develop a public policy for immigration into the United States. Values of providing refuge, protecting citizens, providing opportunities, and building the national and international economies are explored. It will be necessary to define some terms and issues.

Element 3: Taking Positions

(Third class) Students are urged to make decisions and articulate a position with respect to immigration policy. If more than one position is proposed, students are configured to sit with those of like mind. They explain why they have chosen this in relationship to the values defined during the second class.

Argumentation

Element 4: Exploring the Stances Underlying the Positions

(Third and fourth classes) Students are guided and prodded as they explore their stances. They evaluate their position in light of values presented in the second class. They show why their position is best for the country and the world. They discuss possible undesirable consequences of their policy. When values such as providing refuge and protecting citizens come into conflict, students set priorities and make choices.

Element 5: Refining and Qualifying Positions

(Fourth class) Students state their position in regard to U.S. immigration policy along with their rationale. They compare their positions to see strengths and weaknesses of each position in relation to the others.

Element 6: Testing Assumptions About Facts, Definitions, and Consequences

(Fifth class) Several case studies are presented, and students are asked to apply their policy to each case. These include cases of refugees requesting asylum, young families seeking better opportunities (both skilled and unskilled), illegal immigrants who have families involved in the community, people who have family members in the United States and wish to join them, and so on. The students apply their policy to each case.

Sample Socratic Inquiry Lesson:
English Literature—*Frankenstein*

English literature teacher Tanya Perera used the Socratic inquiry model to study the novel Frankenstein.

Objective: Students will analyze the characters of Frankenstein and his monster in Mary Shelley's *Frankenstein*.

Investigation and Analysis

Element 1: Orienting to the Case

Review the novel with the class. Tell the students about Mary Shelley's parents and the fact that some critics think there may be autobiographical pieces in the novel.

Element 2: Identifying the Issues

Draw a table with two columns on the board. Label one column *Frankenstein* and the other *Monster.* Ask students to help fill in the columns with character traits, actions from the novel, and so on. Students should copy this information into their own notes. As the table develops, ask students to be thinking about who is to blame in the novel.

Element 3: Taking Positions

Discuss the table items with students, asking who seems to be more at fault. Ask them how they arrived at these decisions. The teacher should not tell the class who is more to blame, but rather guide the discussion so that students can make a decision for themselves. Tell them each to choose one of the two characters to defend.

Argumentation

Element 4: Exploring the Stances Underlying the Positions

Students break into groups with other students who have chosen the same character to defend. They share with one another why they have chosen this character. Some students may be unsure, so place them in groups so that the groups are fairly equal in number. Students should find specific points in the novel to support their decisions.

Element 5: Refining and Qualifying Positions

The teacher asks students to write down the name of the character they are choosing to defend. They then write two or three reasons they feel this way. Then, they must write two or three reasons why they may be wrong. References to the discussion and the novel must be used. They must also write whether the information regarding Mary Shelley's own life influenced their decisions.

Element 6: Testing Assumptions About Facts, Definitions, and Consequences

Students prepare for a short debate to be held the next day. The debate is to include all the information covered in both the novel and the discussions. After the debate, students write a one- to two-page essay on the topic: "Does it matter who is to blame?" They must decide whether one person's actions excuse the actions of another, or if both must take some responsibility for their behaviors. Support from the novel is needed. This essay will be due the day after the debate.

Sample Socratic Inquiry Lesson: Health Education—Teen Fathers

Following is a lesson plan applying the Socratic inquiry model to a consideration of whether or not teenage fathers should be required to pay child support. The lesson was created by Monica Tourville and taught to 10th- through 12th-grade students with powerful results.

Objective: Students will analyze ethics and present supported opinions as to whether teenage fathers should be required to pay child support.

Investigation and Analysis

Element 1: Orienting to the Case

Facts and Issues: Teacher will research statistics on pregnancy, such as the number of teenage pregnancies, number of teenage mothers on welfare or Women Infants and Children (WIC) assistance, the percentage of teenage parents who drop out of school and never finish versus the percentage who finish, and so on. Teacher provides all these facts and sparks a discussion with students. By prompting and probing, the teacher eventually arrives at the question: Should teenage fathers be required to pay child support?

Element 2: Identifying the Issues

- Policy Issues: This subject involves many policy issues. The teacher must be careful and work hard to keep students on track. Policy issues that might arise surround the question: Because the teenagers are still under 18, who would have to pay—the mother, the father, the state, the grandparents?
- Issue for Discussion: Should teenage fathers have to pay child support?
- Values and Value Conflicts: The teacher sparks discussion regarding different values that come into play. The main focus reverts back to the father's freedom of choice. Can he choose what he wants to do? If he wants the mother to have an abortion or put the baby up for adoption, is he still responsible? Does he have the choice to keep the baby, instead of the mother or her family members? Did he make his choice by consenting to have sex in the first place, so now he simply has to deal with *all* the consequences?
- Underlying Factual and Definitional Questions: When exactly is the cutoff point as to what the father chose to do—when he had sex or when he found out about the pregnancy? Do the father's responsibilities end with the financial aspects, or do they include emotional and physical aspects as well? The teacher discusses all these things with the class, and students arrive at a position.

Element 3: Taking Positions

During this stage, the teacher guides a debate with the students and asks them to take a position on one side or the other. They need to discuss why they are taking this position.

Argumentation

Element 4: Exploring the Stances Underlying the Positions

To engage in debate, students must look at all possible stances, decide at what point a value has been violated, and argue their side while the rest of the class plays devil's advocate.

For an activity, the teacher can divide the class into two or four groups and facilitate the debate. During the debate, the desirable and undesirable consequences of each position must be presented. Desirable consequences might be: both parents staying in school, both getting a part-time job, and both raising the baby. Undesirable consequences might be: the father leaves and abandons all responsibility or the mother drops out of school and remains on welfare or the WIC program.

Some sample questions might be: When exactly are the father's rights violated? Does he have the right to stay in school and finish his education, or does he have to drop out to get a job to pay child support? Can he put off the responsibility until a later date? Can he force the mother to keep the baby against her will? Can she make a decision without him? If he doesn't want the baby, why should he be obligated? What role does the law play in all of this? Can the courts force him to pay support even if he is a teenager? Would his parents then be responsible?

The teacher needs to lead the class to explore all these points and come up with a conclusion on its own. When doing this, students will set priorities, deciding if financial obligations are the most important thing or if the welfare of the baby is more important. The class will need to assert priority of one value over another and demonstrate why the second value is not more important.

Element 5: Refining and Qualifying Positions

At this time, the teacher forces students to take a final stand and state, in their own words, the reasons they have chosen that position. When doing this, students will need to examine a number of similar situations. For example:

Is the baby the most important thing?

Is the baby better off with both parents?

Are both parents physically and mentally healthy and capable of caring for a child?

Is it better to have one functional parent than two dysfunctional parents?

Will the baby make the relationship dysfunctional?

The teacher needs to help students qualify their positions and decide where the responsibilities for the baby will fall.

Element 6: Testing Assumptions About Facts, Definitions, and Consequences

At this point, students will need to revert back to the factual information presented at the very beginning of the lesson. Are these facts relevant? Should they be taken into consideration? When the father does take financial responsibility, does a positive environment result?

Students will also need to state predicted consequences, such as: If the dad is forced to have the baby and assume financial obligations, will he resent it? Will he resent it later on if he doesn't? Will the mother have resentment toward the father and say negative things about him? Will any of this lead to abuse of any of the concerned parties? Will this lead to a great relationship with a lot of love and everything working out? All these consequences need to be predicted, discussed, and examined for validity.

SOCIAL SCIENCE INQUIRY

Similar to cooperative learning and group investigation models, which are discussed in Chapter 7, social science inquiry (Joyce & Weil, 2000) also provides a pattern sometimes followed in Socratic inquiry. Social science inquiry requires three essential characteristics of the reflective classroom:

- Acceptance of all points of view
- Emphasis on hypotheses
- Use of facts as evidence

These elements are necessary if inquiry models are to work.

The Plan

Joyce and Weil (2000) suggest that planning for social science inquiry occurs in six elements: (1) presenting the situation, (2) developing a hypothesis, (3) clarifying the hypothesis, (4) exploring the hypothesis, (5) supporting the hypothesis, and (6) finding a solution.

Element 1: Presenting the Situation

- Present a puzzling situation
- Guide students to clarify the situation

Element 2: Developing a Hypothesis

Have students develop a hypothesis (or hypotheses) from which to explore or solve problems.

Element 3: Clarifying the Hypothesis

Lead students to define and clarify the hypothesis.

Element 4: Exploring the Hypothesis

Guide students in exploring the hypothesis in terms of its assumptions, implications, and logical validity.

Element 5: Supporting the Hypothesis

Ask students to gather facts and evidence to support the hypothesis.

Element 6: Finding a Solution

Facilitate formation of a generalized expression or solution.

Structure of the Learning Climate

The structure of this model is very low level. A teacher may initiate questions or make sure that inquiry moves along, but the students carry responsibility for the development. The teacher needs patience to carry out such a problem-solving approach and the resourcefulness to locate necessary information for which the inquiry may call. Open-ended library resources and access to expert opinion will prove most useful.

Teacher/Learner Interaction

The teacher acts as sharpener, focuser, and counselor to inquiry. Students are thus able to make their ideas clear and enhance their investigation because of these interactions by the teacher.

Outcomes

As the students explore enthusiastically the social questions, they may demonstrate individual interest and commitment to solving certain social problems and improving society. Students are also nurtured by their developing sense of social dignity and their grasp of personal responsibility in dealing with these sorts of problems.

INQUIRY AND LEARNING

There are many ways for the teacher and students to make *inquiry* of knowledge. Parker Palmer (1997) suggests that effective teaching involves both the teacher and the learner as mutual *inquirers* regarding the subject matter. Questions are such a prevalent tool in the hands of all who teach that it is only natural that the questions process would be represented in their patterns of teaching. In the hands of an effective teacher, these models will do more than deliver the subject matter and transform information into personal knowledge. They will teach the learners about lifelong learning itself. The strategies that students use in each of the teaching models discussed above will equip the learners to inquire and find answers regarding any subject they may wish to know about throughout their lives.

QUESTIONING STRATEGIES: A PROCESS FOR TEACHING THROUGH INQUIRY

Much teaching is done with questions. Teachers use questions to assess students' mastery of reading, discussions, and lectures. Questions are the preferred tools for monitoring the level of students' progressive understanding. When they are purposefully linked in a series that focuses the learner on a desired outcome, questions even serve to direct students toward certain understandings. Questions are often interspersed among teacher activities; they are known as *probes* and *reinforcements*.

Teacher silence, which some teachers mistakenly think is undesirable, is also an effective technique. *Wait-time,* as it is now known, occurs when a teacher deliberately and silently pauses before calling for a response to questions that have been posed to students. Teacher wait-time is found in a couple of versions. One is the pause a teacher makes after asking a direct question and before calling on a student or permitting anyone to speak out the answer. Teachers who recognize students by raised hands have an easier time controlling this process than teachers who permit students to simply call out their responses. It is preferred that the teacher explain to the class exactly why he or she wants responses to be offered either by raising hands and waiting to be recognized or by waiting to call out until the teacher has given a recognizable signal. The teacher can explain the process to the learners, letting them know that wait-time gives everyone an opportunity for thoughtful consideration of the question. Thus, students are put on notice that the teacher always expects a *thoughtful response.*

A second strategy for wait-time is found among the probing and prompting techniques used by the teacher. A teacher may accept a partial or lower quality response and then ask other students to assist the first responder. Again, as before, a few seconds should be given for all to process the question. The student who gave the initial response is then permitted to call on another pupil for additional information.

Prompting and Probing for Clarity and Depth

After asking a question, pausing, and calling for or accepting a student's response, the teacher has major decisions to make. Should the student's answer be received, reinforced with a rewarding encouragement, or discouraged with a punishing rebuke? If the response is somewhat incomplete, should the student be prompted to make a more complete answer? Or should the response be probed to extend knowledge for all the learners? Prompting and probing seem to occur almost unconsciously in most teachers' classrooms, as a natural way of reacting to students. Planned use of these techniques, however, can induce much greater success in students' learning.

A prompt is like giving a hint, a part of the response that the teacher wants a student to make. There are three types of prompts:

- Redirecting
- Refocusing
- Hinting or suggesting

A teacher may elect to give a nonresponding student a part of the desired response, a hint. The hint is offered in hopes of jogging the student's memory, leading him or her to remember information that should have been mastered previously. A prompt may also take the form of a second question using different terms to redirect attention, varying the vocabulary to better communicate the question. Or, if a student is off-task or disassociated from the entire frame of reference for the question, the teacher may need to refocus that student to the particular area from which the desired response should be extracted.

A probe is quite different from a prompt. True, the probe may sometimes serve the function of a prompt by revealing to the student an error in judgment or in analysis of the information to be processed. However, probes clarify and elicit higher order thinking skills. They extend understanding among all those listening to the exchange, not the responding learner alone. Probes come in four categories:

- They *clarify* the previous student response.
- They lead to an enhanced *critical awareness* of the previous response.
- They lead students to *relate* one idea to another.
- They help students *predict* eventual outcomes based on the reasoning accumulated in previous responses (see Figure 6.1).

Probes also may redirect the student's erroneous trail of thought onto a path that will lead to more successful conclusions. A student's response to a question may be

- High quality
- Partial or superficial
- Incorrect
- No response

Depending on the nature of that response, the decision to probe or prompt follows. Figure 6.1 outlines possible prompt or probe decisions that a teacher may make for each type of student response. The figure also illustrates a good sequence for questioning.

Questions to Create Higher Order Thinking

Questioning is a primary tool in the teacher's hand for leading students into *higher order* thinking. Students, historically, have been asked many *what* questions—and few *how, why,* or *what do you suppose* questions in relation to educational content. Knowledge requires memory only, repeating information exactly as memorized—the *what.* Comprehension, however, calls for rephrasing, rewording, and comparing information. Application requires the learner to apply knowledge and understanding to determine an appropriate, correct answer. Analysis asks students to identify motives or causes, draw conclusions, or determine evidence. Synthesis leads students to make predictions, produce original communications, or solve problems. Evaluation causes students to make judgments or offer and support opinions.

Figure 6.1 Prompts and Probes

Student Response	Reinforcement Options: Reward/Ignore/Punish	Probe/Prompt Options
High-quality full response	Verbal: "Hmmm..." (pause) "Yes." "That's good!" "Great!" "I like that!" Other forms of praise	Nonprobe Primary probes • Show critical awareness: "Why do you think the way you do?" • Relate: "Can you tie this idea into another?" • Predict: "What do you think will happen?" • Invitation to student to summarize
Partial or superficial response	"Yes, close, but..."	Facilitating prompts • Redirect • Refocus • Hint Primary probes • Clarify: "What do you mean?" • Show critical awareness: "Why do you think the way you do?" • Relate: "Can you tie this idea into another?" • Predict: "What do you think will happen?"
Nonresponse		Silence Facilitating prompts • Redirect • Refocus • Hint

Through a cleverly planned questioning strategy, a teacher can creatively lead students through the cognitive taxonomy of thinking. Carefully devised questions facilitate the observation, communication, comparison, ordering, categorization, relating, inferring from, and application of information. Beginning with *what* or the recall questions, a teacher leads from the knowledge base into understanding, and from understanding into practical application, from application into a more careful analysis, and after analysis, into a synthesis or a reassembling of the notion in a new and different way. This entire process can then be assessed or judged as having merit, quality, or worth, teaching students to evaluate all ideas on a consistent set of criteria.

Many of the verbs and other key words in Figure 3.2 are useful in framing questions that will lead students up the ladder of the cognitive taxonomy. By integrating these key words and phrases to express a specified level of thinking, teachers guide students into higher order thought.

For example, a teacher could promote observation by directing students to "tell us what you see" or to "list the properties that are apparent in the sample." The teacher might ask a question like any of the following:

- What does this look like to you?
- What is the object's size and shape?
- What are the dominant characteristics of this subject?

Selecting key verbs from the application list in Figure 3.2, one could ask a question like

- Can you choose which of the causes of the Civil War we have discussed that would have most affected you if you had lived then?

Applying information or principles, once learned, leads eventually to synthesis of new ideas. Students might be asked

- What political views must be considered if we are to protect the environment of this area?
- What evidence confirms a theory of continental drift?

A next element in the questioning sequence would be a move to the analysis level by inquiring

- Why do you suppose the Northern industrialists were motivated to push for the Civil War?
- Was it truly to free slaves—or might it have been to promote their own economic interests?

Comparing information, the scientific thought process that deals with similarities and differences, makes up a large portion of the analytic questioning that occurs in classrooms. The teacher might ask

- How are these alike?
- How are these different?

A teacher might also suggest that the students compare and contrast, listing both similarities and differences. Still another way to analyze data is the ordering of information in sequence.

- Which came first, second, and last?
- In what order did these events take place?
- Give evidence of a repeating pattern of events.

The teacher may have students analyzing information by category.

- On what basis would you group these ideas or objects?
- What is a different way in which these characteristics can be clustered?
- Why would these items be grouped in this way?

Students can be asked to look for causality of events or information.

- What factors caused this event to occur?
- State this in a testable hypothesis.
- What is the relationship between the coloration of wildlife and its natural habitat?

Following analysis questions, a teacher might wish to ask a synthesis question like

- If you had been the CEO of the largest company back then, but knowing what you know today, how would you have responded? What action would you have taken?
- Use the information you have learned to design something new.
- Invent a glider that will stay in the air longer than anyone else's.
- How might you justify experimentation on animals?
- Create a constitution that truly guarantees individual rights.

The final element in this climb of reason and thought would be leading students into evaluation by asking such questions as these:

- Was it proper for the industrialists to have taken the position that they took? Why or why not?
- Which experimental design was the best? Why?
- Would you vote to adopt this particular proposed constitution, if you were an elected representative of the people? Why or why not?

Related to evaluation is the process of inferring, concluding, and deciding. This is the scientific thinking process that deals with ideas remote in time and space.

- What can be inferred from this information?
- Predict the outcome, and give evidence to support your prediction.
- Under what conditions might we extrapolate from this observed information and believe that a similar reaction could occur under a different circumstance?

SUMMARY

Teachers, questions are your friend! But as with good friend, one must understand how to treat a question with respect and sensitivity. Better stated, one must understand how to treat students with questions sensibly and sensitively. An effective teacher plans questions before the class session, designing them to lead students to higher order thinking. But the teacher also decides in a split second whether to remain silent or to continue the interaction with a reinforcement, a prompt, a primary probe, or a facilitating probe. In the hands of a thoughtful teacher, then, questioning is a powerful tool. Effective teachers, using design-down or backward mapping approaches to lesson design, which were discussed in Chapter 3, will find questions to be an effective ally in cementing student learning as well as in designing lessons around demonstrated student outcomes they envision.

7

The Social Models

Guiding Questions

1. Why are these *social models* so natural to use in serving students?

2. What is *group investigation?* How could you use this model?

3. How is *cooperative learning* different from group investigation?

4. When might be a good time to use a *peer practice* model or strategy?

5. *Nondirective* may be a politically risky term, but how might such an approach be effective for promoting excellent learning outcomes?

The social models combine beliefs about learning and society. Some beliefs about learning see cooperative behavior as both socially and intellectually stimulating. The societal view sees the central role of education as preparing citizens to perpetuate its order, in our case, the democratic social order. Collaboration and cooperation are keys to these models. Teachers are encouraged to remain mindful of the basic philosophical, psychological, and sociological underpinnings of schooling that might be interpreted differently by different social groups. Educational conservatives (including fundamentalists, intellectualists, and the more moderate conservatives) as well as educational liberals (including moderate liberals, liberationists, and anarchists) understand the purpose and practices of schooling from very different points of view (O'Neill, 1990). Social models involve groups and the inquiry process. They call on the teacher to fill more of a facilitator role, whereas group dynamics take over the motivational role. Instructional delivery is deeply embedded within natural social interactions of the participants. The social models herein discussed include *group investigation, cooperative learning* (including *the student teams-achievement divisions strategy* and *the teams-games-tournament strategy), peer practice, role play, simulation, nondirective teaching,* and the *clarification committee model.*

GROUP INVESTIGATION MODEL

The group investigation model is closely tied to the notion of using democratic principles as group operating parameters. It becomes the teacher's role in this process to prepare participants to function effectively within these principles. The basic concepts of inquiry, knowledge, and group dynamics are central to this approach. Investigations range from simple to elaborate. The key element is a challenge or a focus, unleashing the freedom to explore, hypothesize, and select resolutions—elements in common with several other methods as well.

Group investigation has so much in common with cooperative learning that the same planning process may be used for both. This procedure is outlined in the next section.

COOPERATIVE LEARNING MODELS

Learning within cooperative groups is founded on seven basic assumptions. The synergy created in cooperative groups motivates students better than competitive environments. Cooperative groups are greater than the sum of their parts. The sense of connectedness releases high positive energy (Slavin, 1995). Here are some of the distinguishing characteristics of this model, based on (Joyce & Weil, 2000).

- Members of the group learn from each other, and each learner has more helpers than in a direct teaching environment.
- Interaction within the group increases higher order thinking, and learning increases through a combination of cognitive and social complexity.
- Alienation and isolation are minimized through positive group interaction.
- Self-esteem is enhanced.
- Students increase their capacity to work productively in teams.

Cooperative learning takes many forms and may involve any of several different strategies. A particular teacher must create each application of cooperative learning with a particular class in mind. Some strategies work better than others in particular circumstances. Creative teachers give these strategies names such as: pair and share method, numbered heads together, interview method, teams-games-tournaments, Jigsaw, and Jigsaw II (Slavin, 1995).

In these strategies, teachers often organize the class into groups or teams. The teams are regrouped from time to time to avoid problems associated with tracking or permanently grouping learners in a way that subliminally affects their self-esteem and confidence.

Creating Cooperative Learning Groups

When a teacher creates cooperative learning groups, several variables must be considered. If the groups are to be more or less permanent, they should be balanced between males and females. Group members must represent the spectrum of ability levels within the class. If possible, personalities might be considered, so that, for example, not all in a group are outspoken leaders, unwilling to follow others.

On the other hand, temporary groups may appropriately be created based on similarities: language, particular challenges with a concept, or particular readiness for a certain task. In the Jigsaw II strategy, for instance, teachers often select roles for group members in the "expert group" that differ from their roles in their "home team."

The Plan

The general planning outlined below applies to both cooperative learning and group investigation. It involves five elements: (1) encountering a puzzling situation, (2) exploring reactions, (3) organizing for study, (4) completing study, and (5) analyzing progress and process. Also described is the application of these elements in a particular cooperative learning strategy, Jigsaw II. In both cases, the elements are stated in terms of what the *student*, not the teacher, is to do.

General Strategy

Element 1: Encountering a Puzzling Situation (planned or unplanned)

The teacher presents students with materials or information that offers a puzzle or problem needing to be resolved.

Element 2: Exploring Reactions

The teacher probes the students to explore and analyze the information and helps them to collect potential responses and ideas.

Element 3: Organizing for Study

- Formulate study task
- Organize for study by defining the problem, assigning roles and tasks, and so on

Element 4: Completing Study

- Group members complete individual work and report to their groups.
- The group completes its collective analysis.

Element 5: Analyzing Progress and Process

The group next analyzes the process it followed and synthesizes statements about the progress it has made.

Jigsaw II Strategy

Element 1: Encountering a Puzzling Situation

Home team students encounter a puzzling situation (planned or unplanned). Members are assigned (either by the group or by the teacher) to pursue expertise in one component of the puzzling situation.

Element 2: Exploring Reactions

Students move out from home-team groups and come together with similarly assigned colleagues from other teams. They form an "expert group," which pursues an in-depth study of a particular component of the overall learning.

Element 3: Organizing for Study

Experts process assigned information and prepare to return to their home teams to teach their particular portion of the material. Each member of the expert group is sure to become as well prepared as the others because the other home-team members are relying on him or her for this expertise.

Element 4: Completing Study

Experts return to home teams and share information. Each home-team member presents information.

Element 5: Analyzing Progress and Process

Students process the information and prepare to complete the team exercise that the teacher has prepared for this lesson. They evaluate each other's contributions. If team members were remiss in bringing back certain portions of expertise, they are held responsible to the team to find out what is needed and bring it back.

Structure of the Learning Climate

The cooperative learning system is based on the democratic process and group decisions, with low external structure. Puzzlement must be genuine—it cannot be imposed. Authentic exchanges are essential. The atmosphere is one of reason and negotiation. The environment must be able to respond to a variety of learner demands. The teacher and students must be able to assemble what they need when they need it.

Teacher/Learner Interaction

In most cooperative or group learning models and methods, the teacher plays a facilitation role directed at enhancing the group process. The teacher helps learners to formulate plans for action and to manage their own group. The teacher acts as an academic counselor, a guide with suggestions, but not necessarily precise directions or constricting instructions to be followed to the letter.

Outcomes

Instructional outcomes of group processing lessons can lead to a constructivist view of knowledge, disciplined inquiry skills, effective group process, and governance abilities. Nurturing outcomes can be seen in apparent interpersonal warmth and affiliation, commitment to social inquiry, independence as individual learners, respect and dignity for all, and commitment to pluralism. Review the sample lessons that follow; then create a cooperative learning lesson for your class.

Sample Cooperative Learning Lesson (Jigsaw II): Mathematics—Calculator Exploration

Lisa Elliott created the following high school Jigsaw II lesson about calculator exploration to prepare her students to understand uses of the calculator in advanced math for elementary children.

Objective: Students will locate the reciprocal, fraction, parentheses, and exponent keys. They will apply knowledge of these keys in problem solving.

Element 1: Encountering a Puzzling Situation

The teacher introduces the topic as follows: "What if I told you that this calculator could add, subtract, multiply, and divide fractions?" Class discussion follows. The teacher sets the following expectation: "Work in expert teams to analyze the information provided and prepare to explain it to your home team."

Element 2: Exploring Reactions

Students are assigned to home teams. Each home team selects a student to become expert on each of the following calculator keys: exponent, fraction, reciprocal, and parentheses.

Element 3: Organizing for Study

Students work in expert teams, processing the handouts and completing the practice exercises provided by the teacher. Groups prepare to explain the content to their home teams.

Element 4: Completing Study

Members return to their home teams, where each student in turn explains, demonstrates, and teaches the component key process. The home team completes practice exercises provided by the teacher.

Element 5: Analyzing Progress and Process

This lesson concludes with evaluation and team recognition. Each individual in the home team is evaluated on participation, and each team member receives the average worksheet score of his or her group.

STUDENT TEAMS-ACHIEVEMENT DIVISIONS STRATEGY

The student teams-achievement divisions (STAD) strategy is one of the two oldest and most thoroughly researched types of cooperative learning. It is an excellent way to begin using cooperative strategies in developing a collaborative classroom. It consists of five elements: (1) class presentation, (2) teaming, (3) quizzing, (4) individual improvement scoring, and (5) team recognition (Slavin, 1995).

Think of STAD as a track meet with each team member participating in a somewhat different activity appropriate to his or her level. The collective score of the total team decides the outcome. In STAD, each team member is tested against his or her initial performance and rated on improvement. The collective improvement of the whole team decides the outcome and is recognized. The team is the dominant element. Continuous emphasis is placed on the highest and best performance by all team members. Team members are taught to be mutually responsible for the total performance of each team member.

The Plan

Element 1: Class Presentation

- Present material to the class using direct instruction, mastery lecture, Socratic inquiry, or other highly structured and teacher-controlled strategies
- Focus the presentation clearly on the STAD learning unit
- Emphasize that students must pay careful attention because their individual success will assist the team or unit in doing well overall
- Give one to two periods of class instruction

Element 2: Teaming

- Compose teams of four to five students, each team representing a cross-section of the class in academic ability, gender, and ethnicity
- Impress on teams the importance of all members doing well in their individual activity
- After the class presentation, have teams meet and review the advance organizer and other study materials
- Have students discuss identified problems together and compare responses; students should correct any errors or misunderstandings among teammates
- Allow one to two periods of team study time

Element 3: Quizzing

Give individual quizzes. Students may not help each other during the quizzes, but must perform individually.

Element 4: Individual Improvement Scoring

- Set a base score for each team member using the average of his or her previous quiz performances
- Award points to the team for each student's improvement over his or her individual base score

Element 5: Team Recognition

- Give team recognition certificates or other rewards if the team's total scores exceed whatever criterion the teacher has selected
- Awards might be based on a comparison among teams, or a teacher may choose to recognize every team that achieves a certain level of total improvement
- The results of team efforts should be figured and announced immediately after every quiz
- Calculate new base scores
- Team scores may be used as part of an individual student's grades but should never make up more than a small part of the total for any given student (Slavin, 1995, and others recommend a maximum of 20%)

Structure of the Learning Climate

The STAD model is highly structured, with teacher-directed activity and teacher-outlined work periods. Teachers must prepare study materials for pupils to use. Teacher monitoring throughout is essential for team and individual success.

Teacher/Learner Interaction

Teachers interact with the class in the presentation element and with teams during the practice element. Teachers simply monitor during the quiz element and then must critically analyze individual performances. Teachers may find they need to explain to students the analysis of their individual performance and to reiterate the importance of assisting all team members in achieving improvement. It is up to the teacher to build the team—and to build a climate of cooperation in the classroom.

Outcomes

Students come to understand that we are not islands; rather, we are mutually responsible and accountable to others. They begin to accept such responsibility while experiencing the empowerment of assisting the learning of others. As a result, students develop an understanding about the role of teamwork in society, along with mutual self-esteem. Others who are less gifted or exhibit linguistic or other social differences are viewed as members of a mutual learning experience. These are some of the powerful outcomes from continuous application of this model.

TEAMS-GAMES-TOURNAMENT STRATEGY

The Teams-Games-Tournament (TGT) strategy uses the format of the academic tournament in which students compete with representatives from other teams. The competition activity can be used in tandem with the STAD model by substituting the competition for a quiz. TGT is made up of four elements: (1) class presentations, (2) teaming, (3) the gaming tournament, and (4) team recognition (Slavin, 1995).

The Plan

Element 1: Class Presentations

As in the STAD model, Element 1 in TGT consists of a teacher presentation of information, using any of the teacher-directed strategies.

Element 2: Teaming

- Compose teams of four to five students, each team representing a cross-section of the class in academic ability, sex, and ethnicity
- Impress on teams the importance of all members doing well in their individual activity
- Have teams meet after the class presentation and review the advance organizer and other study materials
- Have students discuss the identified problems together and compare responses; students should correct any errors or misunderstandings among teammates
- Allow one to two periods of team study time

Element 3: The Gaming Tournament

- Create questions for the games from the content presented in Element 1
- Design questions to drill and test the knowledge of the participants
- Seat students at tables in threes, one student from each of three different teams
- Have students respond to a question that each selects from the list at their table
- Explain that a challenge rule permits the other two students to question the accuracy of a response

Note: Most games are just questions from a list, but at identified levels of difficulty. Student team members are matched with a question at an appropriate level, based on the student's performance rating. Thus, a student with a high performance rating competes only against other students with a similar rating. A student with a novice performance rating competes against other novices.

The tournament is an overall structure within which different games may occur. It may be conducted at the end of an instructional unit or at the end of an instructional week or month, whichever the teacher determines is best suited to the class curriculum.

Students doing well in their individual performance division in one or more tournaments may be moved up to a higher level of competition for future tournaments. Students not doing well may be moved to less difficult levels. More team points are given for the higher tournament levels of performance, but not so much greater as to invalidate the importance of the lower division student table competitions. Students may compete against each other or, as in STAD, against their previous average individual base score.

Element 4: Team Recognition

Give team recognition certificates or other rewards if the team total scores exceed whatever criterion the teacher has selected. Awards might be based on a comparison among teams, or a teacher may choose to recognize every team that achieves a certain level of total improvement.

Structure of the Learning Climate

Like STAD, the TGT model is highly structured. Teachers prepare study materials for students. Teacher monitoring throughout is essential for success. The teacher arranges the tournaments and recruits people to facilitate them. TGT provides a good opportunity to bring in parents as volunteers (and an excellent opportunity to inform parents about this unique strategy).

Teacher/Learner Interaction

Teachers interact with the class in the presentation element and with teams during the practice element. Teachers monitor some tables during the tournament element, although it is not possible to monitor all the groups. As with all other cooperative learning strategies, the teacher is responsible for building the team and creating a climate of cooperation.

Outcomes

TGT involves competition but requires cooperation among team members to ensure that each member can exceed his or her previous base-level performance. Students must reinforce and practice with one another and accept mutual responsibility for total team outcome. If a team member does not do well in his or her competition, it becomes a challenge for the entire team to make sure the individual member performs well in the next competition.

Like the other cooperative learning strategies, TGT develops teamwork, mutual self-esteem, and acceptance in a mutual learning experience of those who are less gifted or who have linguistic or social differences.

Forming Groups

In TGT and in STAD, as in other cooperative learning methods, care must be taken in forming groups. Teachers must maintain accurate records as to levels of success for each student. Rankings must be given in a way that is challenging but not discouraging to students at the lower levels. Students from each of the ranks must be distributed evenly among all groups.

Likewise, mainstreamed students, learning-handicapped students, ethnic group members, and those who are non-English-speaking or limited-English-proficient should be as evenly distributed as possible. Boys and girls should usually be distributed evenly as well, although occasionally it can be motivational to compete in gender-based groups.

After 6 or 7 weeks, or after each marking period, teams should be reorganized. Teams should never remain together the entire semester or school year.

Sample TGT Lesson (Teams-Games-Tournament): Mathematics—Closed Properties and Sets

Here is a math lesson by Chuck Savage about closed sets, which was built on the TGT version of cooperative learning.

Objective: Students will explain the difference between closed sets and nonclosed sets.

Element 1: Class Presentation

The teacher explains the concept, *the closed property*, using these rules for determining a closed set:

- Must be a specified set
- Operation (addition, subtraction, multiplication, or division) must be specified
- Solution must be a member of specified set

Students work together with the teacher on examples of closed and nonclosed sets in the following:

addition	closed	not closed—for example, $2 + 2 = 4$
subtraction	not closed—for example, $3 - 6$ is not a member	not closed—for example, $0 - 2$ does not result in a member of the set
multiplication	closed	not closed, since $2 \times 2 = 4$, and 4 is not a member
division	not closed—for example, 3/6 is not a member	not closed, since $2/2 = 1$, and 1 is not a member
{3, 6, 9, 12, . . . }	{0, 2}	

Element 2: Teaming

Students form heterogeneously organized study teams for practice. As they practice, these groups ensure that each member knows the concept well. Each team gets a worksheet of 25 sets. Working together, team members determine whether a set is closed or not and explain why there is or is not closure. They check their work with the displayed answers.

Element 3: The Gaming Tournament

Leaving their study teams, students are assigned to tournament tables (four per table) with others of similar ability. Each player rolls a die. The one rolling the highest number begins, followed by the person on his or her left. The player picks a card and answers the problem on the card. Correct answers receive 25 points; incorrect, –25 points. The game continues until the deck is exhausted. Points count only after full rotation to all four players (in the event of time running short). Players add up their scores, record them, and return to their study teams. The study team then adds up the scores of all members and takes an average.

Element 4: Team Recognition

The study team with the highest average receives an award.

PEER PRACTICE MODEL

Peer practice is a process that permits students to become actively involved in self-reinforcement of learning. Students practice a previously taught skill, understanding, or concept by explaining it to their peers while simultaneously reinforcing their helping skills. In the peer practice model, students work in teams of two, fulfilling two roles: *doer* and *helper.*

The task of the doer is to answer questions. The helper provides critical feedback, observing and helping the doer with correctness. The helper also encourages the doer in his or her task. Later, the two exchange roles. The teacher's role throughout this process is to provide tasks that are parallel for the teams, answers to the questions to which the doer must respond, and information that the helper can use in assisting the doer.

The Plan

Planning for peer practice occurs in four elements: (1) preparation; (2) doer/helper, round 1; (3) doer/helper, round 2; and (4) discussion of the roles. These four elements are detailed below.

Element 1: Preparation

- Prepare key questions regarding the material to be reviewed
- Prepare correct answers

- Plan suggested hints and helping ideas that can be used by the helper in assisting the doer
- Present and thoroughly instruct students about the process and the roles

Element 2: Doer/Helper, Round 1

Monitor the doer/helper process:

- Doer reads a question aloud
- Helper makes sure doer understands the question
- Doer attempts to formulate a response
- Helper evaluates doer's response and judges when and how much help to give
- Helper probes, prompts, and guides doer with the helping information prepared by the teacher
- Helper uses supportive feedback to encourage and reinforce doer

Element 3: Doer/Helper, Round 2

Have the helper and doer exchange roles and content.

Element 4: Discussion of the Roles

Lead the class, as a whole or in small groups, in a discussion of the functions they fulfilled in the rounds of the activity and how it helped each to process and master the information.

Structure of the Learning Climate

The teacher structures the process in advance, training the roles thoroughly and always preparing good questions, answers, and information for students to use. The evaluation criteria must demonstrate how the answer was derived, must be self-explanatory, and must be accompanied with positive feedback. Eventually, the structure moves from high-level structure into an almost self-guided level, with the teacher's role merely to set up the information in advance. At some grade levels, the process can become totally self-directed, with students creating their own questions, answers, and helping information.

Teacher/Learner Interaction

In the peer practice model, the teacher plays the preparation and facilitation roles. The teacher helps learner-pairs as they mutually instruct one another. The helper does this by reinforcing the doer as the latter attempts to respond to review questions. In addition, the teacher acts as an academic counselor.

Outcomes

Instructional outcomes enable students to function as partners, to use criteria in judging the quality of responses, and to decide how best to help another. Students develop an effective team process. They strengthen memorization and information-processing skills. Nurturing outcomes are evident through interpersonal warmth and affiliation, independence as learners, team support, and the sense of accomplishment. Students learn to reinforce one another, thus gaining a sense of helping others.

ROLE-PLAYING MODEL

In the role-playing model, students adopt character roles related to certain human relations problems. They create and act out the dialogue that might accompany such a situation. This helps students to create personal meaning with the information that accompanies the story of a given problem or social issue. They can safely express their deeply guarded personal views as they *try out* certain responses. The information or lesson material for use in such a lesson can come from literature, history, sociology, family life, or even from some of the so-called *hard science* subjects.

The Plan

Joyce and Weil (2000) have outlined these nine elements for role playing: (1) warming up the group, (2) selecting participants, (3) setting the stage, (4) preparing the observers, (5) enacting the role-play, (6) discussing and evaluating, (7) reenacting, (8) discussing and evaluating again, and (9) sharing experiences and drawing generalizations. These are outlined below.

Element 1: Warming Up the Group

- Identify or introduce the problem
- Make the problem explicit
- Interpret the problem story and explore issues
- Explain the process of role-playing

Element 2: Selecting Participants

- Lead students to analyze roles
- Select role-players

Element 3: Setting the Stage

- Set the line of action
- Restate the roles
- Help students get inside the problem situation

Element 4: Preparing the Observers

- Lead students to decide what to look for
- Assign observation tasks

Element 5: Enacting the Role-Play

- Begin and maintain role-play
- Break role-play when the desired stage of observation and awareness has been achieved

Element 6: Discussing and Evaluating

- Lead students to review the action of the role-play
- Guide discussion of the major focus
- Help students develop the next enactment

Element 7: Reenacting

- Have students reverse roles
- Suggest next elements or behavioral alternatives

Element 8: Discussing and Evaluating Again

- Lead class discussion of the role enactments
- Probe for understandings and revelations

Element 9: Sharing Experiences and Drawing Generalizations

- Facilitate discussion as students relate the problem situation to real experience and current problems
- Guide exploration of general principles of behavior

Structure of the Learning Climate

The role-playing model is moderately structured. The teacher is responsible for initiating the elements and guiding students through the activities within each element. The students largely determine the particular content of the discussions and enactments. Role-playing is an experience-based model and requires minimal support material outside of the initial problem situation.

Teacher/Learner Interaction

In role-play, the teacher should accept all student responses in a nonevaluative manner. The teacher is present to help students explore various sides of the problem situation and compare alternative views. The teacher wants to increase students' awareness of their own views and feelings by reflecting, paraphrasing, and summarizing their responses. Continually referring to the concept of role, the teacher emphasizes that there are different ways to play a role and that there are alternative ways to resolve a problem.

Outcomes

Instructional outcomes of role-play help learners consider their personal values and actions. They can also create approaches for solving relationship problems similar to their own or those of their peers. When students develop an understanding about chronic relationship problems or values, they are nurtured by being able to safely express themselves.

SIMULATIONS MODEL

Simulations employ goal orientation as a stimulus for learning. They depend on constructs, frames of reference, software, and an introduction emphasizing the necessity of solving problems along the way toward goal attainment. Much of the learning is conscious, but significant portions are actually subliminal. Originating from the field of cybernetics, simulations have been increasingly applied to classroom learning over the past 30 years. Several key strengths for teaching and learning are available through the simulations model. Real-world learning tasks may be effectively simplified, controlled, and yet introduced into a multiplicity of alternate instructional models for any number of learning purposes. Simulations permit students to learn from self-generated feedback, a strategy with proven effectiveness.

The Plan

Bruce Joyce (Joyce & Weil, 2000) suggested that a teacher might prepare a simulation in four elements, as detailed below. The four elements are (1) orientation, (2) participant training, (3) simulation operations, and (4) participant debriefing.

Element 1: Orientation

- Present the broad topic of the simulation and the concepts to be incorporated into the simulation activity at hand
- Explain simulation and gaming
- Give an overview of the simulation

Element 2: Participant Training

- Set up the scenario: rules, roles, procedures, scoring, types of decisions to be made, and goals
- Assign roles
- Hold abbreviated practice sessions

Element 3: Simulation Operations

- Conduct the game activity and supervise its administration
- Provide feedback and evaluation of the performance and effects of the decisions
- Clarify misconceptions
- Continue simulation

Element 4: Participant Debriefing

Guide students as they engage in any or all of the following:

- Summarize events and perceptions
- Summarize difficulties and insights
- Analyze the process
- Compare simulation activity to the real world
- Relate simulation activity to course content
- Appraise and redesign the simulation (Joyce & Weil, 2000)

Structure of the Learning Climate

In the simulations model, the social system is structured by the teacher through selecting materials and directing the particular simulation. The interactive environment of the class, however, should be nonthreatening and marked by cooperation. The teacher manages the simulation, explains the game, maintains the rules, coaches, and conducts the debriefing. Simulation requires a carefully structured base of resource materials, instructional settings, and real-life situations.

Teacher/Learner Interaction

In simulations, the teacher's roles include explaining, refereeing, coaching, and guiding discussion, as well as developing the overall simulation plan and monitoring group progress. In a simulation, teachers must not evaluate players' decisions and moves. Students will receive and apply the lesson rules or procedures best when they have been encouraged with expressions of safety and trust. When necessary, the teacher must move students forward with the activity.

Outcomes

Instructional outcomes in simulation teaching include knowledge of new concepts and skills, understanding of political and economic systems, and transferable insight gained by students. Students are nurtured in their personal awareness of these new learnings, including critical thinking, decision making, empathy, awareness of the role of chance, and facing consequences. They have an enhanced sense of effectiveness.

Sample Simulation Lesson: U.S. History—The Constitutional Convention

Following is a lesson plan applying the simulation model to the Constitutional Convention. The lesson was created by Karen Earl. Note that the lesson uses an advance organizer, borrowed from the behavioral models, and omits a second enactment because the purpose here is to understand the Constitutional Convention as it actually happened, not to suppose how it might have been changed.

Objective: Students will demonstrate knowledge and understanding of the U.S. Constitution in simulating the Constitutional Convention.

Materials: Descriptive materials and transcripts of convention, detailed listings of members, evaluation sheets

Element 1: Advance Organizer

An outline and chart are distributed and explained to students. These materials (1) place the Constitutional Convention in historical perspective; (2) emphasize the weakness of the original Confederation, citing the need for a stronger form of government; (3) explain that two representatives from each colony are to meet for the purpose of constructing the new government framework.

Element 2: Orientation

Say: "We are going to enact the Constitutional Convention. Each of you will assume the role of a colonial representative in order to discover what this process was like. The simulation will take several days and will cover the events as they unfolded at the daily meetings. Grading will be based on attentiveness to sessions and thoroughness in researching assigned roles. A sheet reflecting daily cumulative points scored will be kept at my desk for your information."

Element 3: Participant Training

Room arrangement is discussed. Parliamentary procedure is explained and practiced. Scoring methods and day-to-day procedures are presented and explained.

The teacher checks understanding thoroughly. George Washington's role is filled by election. The student Washington is given additional instructions to conduct sessions. Other roles are to be worked out by students by researching transcripts and other text materials. The room is rearranged and a brief practice session is conducted.

Element 4: Simulation Operations

Washington is in charge of the convention. The teacher is a resource person standing by to clarify misconceptions and provide feedback. The simulation runs for several days. The teacher provides daily activities for Washington to suggest to the convention and gives students daily feedback on their participation scores. If students ask, they receive assistance in locating and processing historical information that will assist them in addressing the daily task.

Element 5: Participant Debriefing

At the end of the simulation, students summarize any problems and/or insights they have experienced. They analyze the process in class and discuss new understandings of the development of the Constitution and its meaning for us today. Written evaluation forms are distributed and completed by the students.

Element 6: Feedback and Evaluation

Evaluation sheets are used by the teacher to assess student performance and to upgrade the project for future class applications.

THE NONDIRECTIVE TEACHING MODEL

Nondirective teaching is a model drawn from several strategies that could be classified as personal learning (Joyce & Weil, 2000). Personal learning strategies lead students toward greater mental and emotional health by improving the concept of self, increasing realism, creating self-confidence, and extending sympathetic and empathetic reactions to others. Such strategies increase the proportion of education that emanates from the needs and aspirations of the students themselves, taking each student as a partner in determining the content and process for learning.

Based on the work of Carl Rogers (1982), nondirective teaching focuses on facilitating learning. The primary goal is to assist students in attaining greater personal integration, effectiveness, and realistic self-appraisal. It may be used for problem-solving situations dealing with personal, social, or academic issues. To use nondirective teaching effectively, a teacher must be willing to accept that a student can understand and cope with his or her own life. The teacher shall not judge the student. The teacher does not diagnose the problem but rather attempts to perceive the student's world as the student perceives it. Implementation of this method is likely to bring some criticism from the parent community. It is important that the teacher and administrator thoroughly communicate with parents prior to implementation.

The Plan

Bruce Joyce illustrates a nondirective teaching model through five elements: (1) defining the helping situation, (2) exploring the problem, (3) developing insight, (4) planning and decision making, and (5) integrating (Joyce & Weil, 2000).

Element 1: Defining the Helping Situation

Help students to express feelings accurately without judgment.

Element 2: Exploring the Problem

Help the learners with probes and prompts to express and define terms accurately.

Element 3: Developing Insight

- Stimulate the discussion among the learners and extend it
- Lead the learners to articulate and support their conclusions

Element 4: Planning and Decision Making

- Monitor student discussions and facilitate them as they make conclusions
- Encourage learners to clarify their original ideas

Element 5: Integrating

Prompt learners to transfer the idea to new applications.

Structure of the Learning Climate

The structure for this model is very low—in fact, *nonexistent,* some would say. Students initiate interest in problem-based areas of learning, and the teacher facilitates their process of investigation. There is no use of behavioral concepts like reward and punishment. Students are rewarded through their accomplishment of learning and satisfaction of questions raised. The teacher needs a quiet, private place for individual contacts; a larger center for group conferences; and a resource center from which students may draw materials that will meet their instructional objectives.

Teacher/Learner Interaction

The teacher reaches out to students, empathizes, and reacts in ways that help students define problems and take action to achieve solutions.

Outcomes

Although the outcomes of nondirective teaching may be honestly debated among educational professionals, some would say that the instructional outcomes of this model are nil. Others cite attainment of the skills, abilities, and concepts outlined in the instructional objective undertaken by the students. Most would agree that the nurturing outcomes include personal awareness, self-development, and a variety of social and academic goals.

CLARIFICATION COMMITTEE MODEL

The clarification committee model is drawn from Socratic inquiry and research by Parker Palmer (1993) on Quaker practices. The model involves three elements: (1) definition of the problem, (2) clarification through questioning by the committee, and (3) culmination.

The Plan

Element 1: Definition of the Problem

Have an individual student

- Pose a problem, issue, or concern
- Develop a thorough but succinct review of the issue and background

Element 2: Clarification Through Questioning by the Committee

- Have the individual select a committee
- Facilitate and monitor the committee as it reviews the paper
- Listen to an oral presentation
- Ask questions of the presenter, but refrain from giving information, opinions, or ideas
- Listen to the individual's responses and perhaps ask more questions

Element 3: Culmination

- Record the committee process
- The individual reviews and develops a solution statement

Structure of the Learning Climate

The process has little external structure and is controlled by the student. However, the process is very demanding. It requires that the committee focus on listening and abandon any tendency to give advice.

Teacher/Learner Interaction

The teacher facilitates and coaches the process.

Outcomes

The process is startling. As the committee proceeds, possible solutions to the problem are clarified as coming from within the learner. The questions simply serve to reveal or uncover the answer.

ON TO THE COLLABORATIVE CLASSROOM

The notion of a collaborative classroom is a little different from cooperative learning. Cooperative learning goes on *within* a collaborative classroom, along with many other strategies. What should the collaborative classroom look like?

The learning of one student relates to the learning of other students. In contrast, many classrooms are competitive. Students may do simple group work, but there is no linkage. In such a classroom young people become individualistic, atomistic, and usually self-centered. All students have a sense of mutual ownership of the classroom. The atmosphere is secure, safe, accepting, and mutually supportive. Students do not feel afraid of the teacher. Gifts, talents, interests, and individual differences are mutually encouraged. Development of specific servanthood skills is a must. Students are taught to respond in service through caregiving, stewardship, healing, reconciliation, and peace making. Students are taught to be respectful of others.

In addition to cooperative and collaborative teaching strategies, a collaborative classroom involves learners together with teachers in making decisions. Teachers collaborate with students about grades, about strategies for helping students maximize improvement, and about desired performances by students. Teachers frequently use collaborative conferences with individual learners to discuss performance on various demonstrations or projects. Learning, to be retained, must be meaningful to each individual student; this cannot be achieved in whole class-directed instruction. It can only be accomplished by a teacher and a student working one-on-one. While cooperative team activities are under way, teachers may find opportunities to conduct individual collaborations with students.

Much time is taken to make this part of the collaborative classroom work. Students cannot miss important practice time with their teams, nor performance time. Students must feel attentive and comfortable in the collaborative conference. Students must prepare for the collaborative conference with a self-analysis of their performance to date. Teachers then guide the student toward improved performance with suggestions, inquiry, and probing. Not all students are able to make these judgments, so teachers must be prepared for different levels of collaboration within a given class group.

8

The Writing Process as a Teaching Model

Guiding Questions

1. What is process writing and how might effective teachers use it to enhance student learning outcomes?

2. Prewriting activities are important enough to be carefully planned. How might you use elements of some instructional models already discussed in this phase of a writing process lesson?

3. What are some of the categories of process writing applications?

4. How might process writing steps be integrated into an actual lesson plan?

5. What is a scoring rubric, and how would you use it to assess writing products from students?

6. When building a rubric for a writing process lesson, why might it be important to engage the learners in discovering and owning the rubric elements, even though this takes more time?

Writing is an integral part of the English language arts and of most other curriculum areas. It is often said that writing is the most difficult language arts component to develop. Students usually have a large receptive, but a smaller expressive, vocabulary. The latter is the resource for written expression.

Writing involves both composing and transcribing. To compose, students need to understand relationships between words and thoughts. In composing, a writer first selects and orders words into patterns to express his or her ideas. Transcribing is the process of setting the word patterns on paper so they are readily understandable to a reader. The elements or stages in writing make up the *writing process*. This formalized process is easy to follow and contains built-in procedures to assist teachers in responding to student writing in ways that are both positive and instructional.

At all grade levels, it is *necessary* that teachers both teach and review standard grammar, syntax, spelling, and mechanics. Involving the students in editing written work with the use of editorial marks and notations enhances instruction in these areas. Often, after targeted instruction, written activities may focus on particular aspects of grammar, syntax, or mechanics, and the evaluation of student outcomes is directed according to student needs.

Since the early 1970s, research and development for classroom writing has been ongoing by the National Writing Project, arguably the most significant project of its kind in North American schools. It created and disseminated a professional development model about teaching writing that has been implemented in every state of the nation. In local schools, districts, county offices of education, and staff development centers, generations of classroom teachers have been introduced and coached into writing process steps and uses. Over time, the patterns for writing process themselves became a widely used model for teaching involving writing. Every student can learn to write passably and clearly. Not all will be gifted writers, but all can communicate in writing with facility and ease. All students deserve a teacher who is skilled at teaching them to use a process for written communication to successful ends.

PRACTICAL APPLICATIONS FOR WRITING PROCESS LESSONS

It is most important that students discover writing as a key to lifelong communication. Writing must not be mysterious, theoretical, or difficult to accomplish. There are many practical applications that we can put before learners as activities in which they will *want* to write correctly and well. Letters to friends are a good place to start. Help pupils to understand the importance of clear, concise, and correct communication to avoid misunderstanding with their close friends and relatives. From friendly letters, the teacher may next branch into business letters, letters of application for jobs or scholarships, and other business writing tasks for which students may have some need. Writing interview questions and responses is an interesting task that might elicit keen attention and careful and thoughtful reflection on written communiqués.

TEACHING MODELS AS WRITING STARTERS

The writing process may be combined with any teaching model if students are to produce a written output. The concept formation models discussed earlier in this book are particularly useful as vehicles for prewriting and responding. Simulation, role-playing, and synectics can also be applied to stimulate and assist written communication. An important key for the teacher is to make certain that students understand those teaching models when they are used in writing lessons. In this way, the teaching models can become tools for students to use in improving their own communication.

TYPES AND CATEGORIES OF WRITING

In most school districts, writing process programs have been organized to evaluate the success of student writing. Particular forms of writing are evaluated at specified grade levels. Below are brief descriptions of different types of writing that may be taught and assessed in your state.

Autobiographical Incident

The autobiographical incident is a well-told story about a specific occurrence in the writer's life. It uses vivid sensory details, includes some indication of the significance of the event, and allows the reader to share some of the writer's feelings. The writer most commonly (a) chooses a significant incident in his or her life; (b) describes the place, the people, and the events that make this incident significant; (c) focuses on self, creating an artistic statement; and (d) deals honestly with his or her feelings about the experience.

What Good Writers of an Autobiographical Incident Do

Detail the significant scene and people

Establish clearly the event's importance

Organize chronologically

Use an interest-catching introduction

Write in the first person

Employ both description and narration

Firsthand Biography/Sketch

The firsthand biography/sketch reveals another person through the writer's eyes and shows the writer's response to that person. The narrative may be either true or wholly imaginative, as in fantasy or fictionalized life experiences. Stories typically involve plot, conflict, sequence, point of view, dialogue, action, and description.

Report of Information

The report of information calls on a writer to gather, organize, and report information collected from a number of sources. The writer must arrange and report information clearly around a thesis or key idea, while holding the reader's interest and supporting the thesis with appropriate evidence or details. Common characteristics include (a) a thesis or main focus; (b) an appeal to the interests of the readers; (c) clear definitions of important words, terms, and phrases; (d) an opening that describes how the report is organized; and (e) successful elaboration on the thesis idea supported with explanation, evidence, and well-structured details.

What Good Report Writers Do
Select a topic that is both interesting and usable
Communicate a particular point of view
Develop the information by using classification, comparisons and contrasts, and narration
Organize the information logically and coherently

Analysis: Speculation About Cause and Effect

The analytic paper involving speculation about causes and effects asks a writer to predict possible outcomes or consequences of a given situation, event, or trend. Common characteristics include (a) an introduction proposing a trend or incident of interest to the target audience; (b) consideration of various possible causes, drawing on statistics, anecdotes, and authoritative information; and (c) an authoritative voice.

What Good Analytical Writers Do
Distinguish clearly between remote causes and immediate causes
Provide a list and analysis of the causes of the particular subject
Detail the causes with supportive facts, as well as with anecdotes and authoritative information
Identify the more important causes
Mitigate possible arguments from a reader with logical refutation

Reflective Essay

A reflective essay focuses on exploration and discovery rather than on final thoughts. It is an open, natural, and intimate reflection derived from personal experience. A reflective writer works to see connections between experience and idea, to test out that idea in the light of other experiences, and to arrive at new dimensions of the original thought. Reflection creates insights, and possibly a change in the writer's worldview. A thoughtful voice and style demonstrate a sense of genuine involvement in the ideas presented. Common characteristics include (a) a general observation about human existence drawn from a significant personal event, (b) narration of the event using sensory language and details, and (c) writing in the first person.

What Good Reflective Essayists Do

Place the significance of the personal event in a larger context

Cite parallels between specific behaviors and general human nature

Show, not tell

Describe vividly with imagery, including similes, analogies, and metaphors

---

Evaluation

A written evaluation states a position or judgment on the worth of some object, book, movie, product, or idea and attempts to validate this position with evidence and examples. Qualitative analysis, judgment, and clear criteria of unquestioned logic are represented in the writer's work. The common characteristics of evaluation writing are (a) stated or implied judgment as the major point; (b) perhaps a description of the subject; (c) a convincing argument, possibly using comparison and contrast to prove the judgment; (d) an organized presentation of the evidence; and (e) a stated awareness that the judgment is the writer's own opinion.

What Good Writers of Evaluation Pieces Do

Begin by addressing their audience

Describe the subject clearly

Explain the evidence

Provide examples to illustrate the evidence

Establish a particular tone or attitude toward the subject

Arrange reasons and examples logically

Explain the judgment, rationale, and conclusions

Interpretation

Interpretation demonstrates a writer's claims about the meaning of an idea, event, phenomenon, or object. Point of view and perspective are clearly presented and distinguished from other possibilities. Evidence and criteria remain clear components of these compositions. Although similar to evaluation in that it presents a judgment built on criteria, an interpretive judgment is based on *non-standardized* criteria. The writer carefully studies facts, data, and observations on a subject. A stand is taken as to causes or effects of the phenomenon. Because the writer's interpretation is supported with reasons and studied evidence, the reader becomes persuaded that the writer's meaning is correct.

What Good Interpretation Writers Do

State meaning clearly

Develop the argument logically

Provide a rationale for the interpretation, supported by facts, data, and observations tied together in a cohesive manner

Write convincingly

Transition effectively

Controversial Issue

A controversial issue piece allows students to examine complex problems, to take positions after thoughtful deliberation, and then to defend these positions by constructing well-reasoned arguments. Writers strive to understand their readers' values and assumptions in order to establish common ground for reasoned argument. A writer presents a clearly defined issue and then takes an authoritative stand concerning that issue. Often, the writer must develop multiple perspectives on the issue, reflecting support and opposition. The writer supports his or her position with logical and relevant evidence.

What Good Writers on Controversial Issues Do

Present evidence in a logical progression

Anticipate concerns or objections and disprove them

Address the reader directly

Establish credibility with the reader

Observational Writing

Observational writing focuses on a person, group, or event to be objectively re-created in words and interpreted or reflected on by the witnessing writer.

To see or observe something involves both a transition of the sensory act into words and an interpretation of that act in view of the rest of reality. Through analysis, synthesis, and evaluation, a writer sorts out cause-effect relationships, draws inferences, and states conclusions.

THE PROCESS OF WRITING

There are very clear elements that, when followed, enable students to write successfully and clearly. This formalized process is referred to as the writing process, or as *process writing.*

Process writing consists of five basic stages:

1. Prewriting

2. Composing, writing, or drafting

3. Responding or peer responding

4. Revising

5. Editing

Many authorities add a sixth stage, *postwriting,* which includes evaluation and publishing activities. Some authorities insert yet another stage called *teaching enabling language skills,* making an eight-stage process, as shown below.

Different Descriptions of the Writing Process

The Five-Stage Process Description

Prewriting	Composing	Responding	Revising	Editing

The Six-Stage Process Description

Prewriting	Composing	Responding	Revising	Editing	Publishing

The Eight-Stage Process Description

Prewriting	Writing	Responding	Revising	Enabling language skills	Editing	Evaluating	Publishing

---

The National Writing Project (CDE, 1990) has developed the writing process framework shown below. This framework is followed in the remainder of this chapter as we present the writing process as a model of teaching.

The National Writing Project's Framework					
Prewriting	Writing	Sharing	Revising	Editing	Evaluating

THE PROCESS OF WRITING AS A TEACHING MODEL

We've heard it said and seen it in print in many authoritative documents: *All teachers teach writing.* Regardless of age level, regardless of subject focus, writing is a major communication skill, second only to speaking in most cultures. Thus, to be a successful communicator, our students must learn to be effective writers. This, of course, involves much more than teaching forms or styles of penmanship. Good writers communicate their ideas effectively and efficiently so that they can be understood. If I teach students to understand certain algebraic concepts in a math lesson, eventually, they may have to write about that concept and explain it, whether in an examination or in another forum. Their use of written language skills will be essential in getting the conceptual understanding out of their mind and communicating it to others.

The Plan

Teaching all students well means you teach them to write, regardless of what else you are assigned to teach. All classes can and should have lessons that involve writing processes. Thus, it serves all teachers to become masters of process writing. Process writing comes from the collective efforts of the National Writing Project (n.d.) across the past 30 years.

In planning for a writing activity, a teacher thinks through each element of the writing process framework in relation to the particular type of writing that is desired for students to master and use. There are several writing types that can be selected for use, but all types of writing make use of the same framework: prewriting, writing, sharing/responding, revising, editing, evaluating, and publishing.

Element 1: Prewriting

Prewriting activities are designed to stimulate the flow of ideas before any structured writing begins. They include outlining, webbing, clustering, brainstorming, mapping, concept construction, debating, free writing, fantasizing, and other such strategies.

A word about clustering: Findings from the past 20 years of brain research have produced various prewriting strategies that we can generically refer to as *clustering.* The logic-ordered left brain interacting with the right hemisphere of the brain and its holistic image making and synthesizing capabilities facilitates

Figure 8.1 Clustering

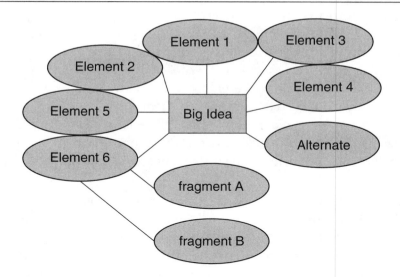

a truly effective writing effort. Writing tends to move from the (possibly vague) whole into parts—then back into a new and enhanced whole.

Clustering creates a web of intersecting bubbles of elements taken from the idea of the whole. Figure 8.1 illustrates how a "big idea" can become linked to several of its component elements and related concepts. Such graphic organizers help visual students to grasp the relationships within and among concepts and terms. These elements are then organized or reorganized for better understanding. The new whole is fashioned from the outline established by the new clusters and their components. Clustering supports a type of nonlinear thinking sometimes called brainstorming.

A web gradually takes shape as students collectively share ideas and observed relationships. Ideas can be adjusted, moved, and reassociated with other ideas until a diagram of a possible theme becomes apparent. Classes can be taught this strategy, and it can be practiced in small groups. Eventually, individual learners make use of clustering to stimulate and delimit topics about which they might be writing.

Another graphic organizer for clustering is a tree story with a "main idea" trunk and the ever-branching elements of the story. Graphic organizers can be as simple as sets of boxes or circles—or as complex as interlinking shapes to illustrate intersecting ideas. The process of graphically organizing information brings right and left brain into sync on a particular idea for greater understanding and higher creativity.

Element 2: Writing (Composing or Drafting)

Students give shape to ideas by composing their thoughts in writing. Writing is, then, a discovery on the conscious level. Writers "let go" and disappear into the act of writing. This is a first draft, never evaluated for correctness, format, structure, or even content.

Element 3: Sharing and Responding

Given a chance to share with others, writers gain a sense of the power with which their words impact others. They acquire a sense of audience through a "trusted other." From responses by a listener or a reader, the writer discovers whether the audience hears what the writer intended to write. The responder asks if the message could be clearer, more descriptive, and so on. The writer takes careful notes on corrections and ideas from peers.

Teachers may wish to create a revision guide for students' use. The guide may be generic in nature or specific to one of the major types of writing. Such a guide might include the following instructions for students:

- In your own words, summarize this writer's position on the issue.
- Reread the introduction, then tell what it does to get the reader immediately involved.
- What additional information would you like to know about the subject?
- In your own words, list the key ideas contained in this writing.
- Is the conclusion supported by the rest of the piece?

One particularly useful strategy to introduce in the peer response element of writing process lessons is the read-around groups. In this process, students are grouped in small teams and prepared to work constructively together. Team members are given each other's papers and asked to read them, writing concise comments about content, flow, and structure—but not editing for spelling, punctuation, or grammar. The teacher allows a very brief period of time, say three minutes, for the first reading, and then, on a signal, the papers are rotated to the next group member to read. This continues until all team members have read and commented on the papers of all other members. Finally, the papers go back to the authors, who are given a period to ask questions to clarify the responses of their teammates.

Element 4: Revising

Element 4 calls for a review of the writing in light of the feedback. It is a reworking of the composition on both semantic and lexical levels. The writer is concerned with both the chosen words and how those words work together. At this stage, the student deletes, adds, rephrases, revises, and then produces a second draft.

Element 5: Editing

This is the stage at which standard format is imposed on syntax, grammar, spelling, punctuation, paragraphing, sequence, and flow of language. Editing clarifies the written message. During this stage of alteration and refinement, a teacher is asked to use linguistic expertise, assisting the student with correctness of the composition. Often, this stage can be integrated with instructional lessons in specific areas of grammar, structure, or syntax. The teacher is then able to draw on students' own writing, instead of arbitrary grammar exercises, to illustrate polishing techniques.

The read-around group, described above as a technique for sharing and responding, is also appropriate for peer editing, except that students are given a longer, but still limited time to proofread and highlight areas that need technical attention.

Element 6: Evaluating

The evaluation stage assigns value and worth to the product. Evaluation may involve grades, but it is usually much more. After spending this much time with a piece of writing, a student's self-image becomes tied up with the product. Here, teachers must not casually impose arbitrary assessments on student work. It is best if the students know in advance and agree with the standards used to evaluate their writing. Authentic or holistic assessment (discussed below) is gaining widespread interest and use as an approach to evaluate student writing.

Here, as in sharing and editing, read-around groups are valuable. Team members can be led through application of a standard rubric, after which each student holistically scores the other students' papers. In this way, students can benefit from mutual feedback, and the teacher is not continuously saddled with the task of editing stacks and stacks of student papers.

Structure of the Learning Climate

Process writing models may be delivered in any environment, from high to low structure. One principal aim of process writing is that students internalize the process to the extent that they will almost instinctively follow it. The teacher generally initiates the process and sees that it moves from element to element. Students, however, carry the responsibility for its development. The social norms call for open discussion among equals. The teacher needs patience to permit students the time necessary to develop their theses as well as resourcefulness in guiding students to locate necessary information. Open-ended library resources and access to expert opinion may also be required.

Teacher/Learner Interaction

The teacher gives initial direction and establishes time parameters. Students are usually empowered to work in small groups or pairs for mutual assistance. The teacher quickly moves out of the directive role and into the role of facilitator.

Outcomes

Instructional outcomes are seen as students become more skillful in written communication, understanding different approaches appropriate to varying circumstances. Students are nurtured to acquire confidence in representing their thoughts through written communication.

EVALUATION OF WRITING: HOLISTIC SCORING STRATEGIES

Like anything that is taught, writing must be evaluated and feedback given in ways that lead to personal growth in skills and abilities. Traditional evaluation of writing consisted of an essentially subjective process. Teachers assigned a letter grade based on their judgment as to the content and the process involved in a student's performance on the writing exercise. There may have been an attempt to objectify the process by creating and presenting to students a set of characteristics of exemplary or preferred accomplishment on the activity. These characteristics were then translated into the traditional A to F grading system of American education. Within the past two decades, however, the concept of holistic scoring has arisen as a more meaningful way of evaluating student writing.

The wide divergence among the many sets of "preferred conditions" that teachers had developed perhaps contributed to interest in the holistic approach. In holistic scoring, quality points are allotted to a piece of writing based on its identifiable qualities as compared against a rubric. A rubric consists of a set of criteria or conditions that describes, in descending degrees, the qualities that should or might be attained in the finished written exercise. Holistic scoring must be explained to students. When possible, students should be involved in creating the rubric, thus ensuring that they have an understanding of the most desirable conditions to be achieved.

Please refer to Appendices A and B for sample rubrics for K to 8 and secondary writing instruction and evaluation. The special benefit of using rubrics is that the evaluation process may be molded and targeted to different purposes, tasks, types of writing, and/or writing foci.

Teachers using rubrics will want to involve the students in the rubric application. As the particular desired learning foci are laid out during direct instruction or through one of the indirect information-processing models, the teacher will want to put the rubric in front of the students. It may be helpful to make use of inquiry model lesson elements at this point and guide students into discovering or creating the rubric that the teacher has in mind. Thus, in teaching about the rubric, the teacher is either introducing new learning or reviewing skills already learned.

A Teacher's Experience—Peer Editing

Edith was teaching an intermediate math lesson about rudimentary algebraic concepts. The students completed the text chapters, and Edith wanted to organize a math competition. One of the activities she devised was to have students draw a card naming a concept and then explain it to a partner. The partner would then write an explanation of the concept on a judging sheet. The pair received points based on how well the partner wrote out the explanation. In preparation for the math fair day, the teacher had students review the vocabulary list from their math chapter and then write out explanations of each major concept. She decided to use the writing process for two class sessions (about 55 minutes in a self-contained class day) with the competition day being on the third day in class.

After the students had reviewed the vocabulary terms in the chapters, Edith gave them 3 × 5 cards and asked them to label one concept on each card. Then, she had them write down the concept explanation as she called each out. Afterward, Edith asked them each to share the card with their partner, who was to point out suggestions for making the response completely clear. The students were to then revise their cards to best express their concepts.

In the second class period, the teacher had the pair switch cards with another pair and use peer editing responses. The editors were to cite page numbers from the text if they marked something as needing change. The cards were then returned, and the authors rewrote their cards to most accurately express their terms.

In the third class session, the math competition was held, with points given for the accuracy of the partner's written response. This was the first time the teacher saw the written responses from the students.

A Teacher's Experience—Peer Editing and Revising

Another teacher, Chuck Savage, was teaching a physical education unit on soccer to eighth graders. Chuck taught the basic rules, and the students played the game for several days. During a bad weather day (which happened quite regularly in their region of the country), Chuck had the students write a two-page essay explaining the game of soccer to a person who knew nothing about it. The lesson began with a prewriting activity using concept development and creating a web of topics and ideas about the game of soccer. The prewriting activity concluded with the formation of a rubric for an accurate description of the game called soccer. The students next wrote their drafts as a homework activity and returned the next day for the subsequent activity. After the writing phase, the students switched papers with each other and responded as to the clarity and accuracy of their peers' ideas. The responders were not to correct anything but merely to point out where there was a problem or where the written language was not clear. The students spent the remainder of the class period revising their papers. The teacher then announced that this would be the unit exam on soccer but that they would not be doing any further peer editing steps. The students had the option of turning the papers in as they had been revised or taking them home one more night and reviewing against the materials Chuck had distributed at the beginning of the soccer unit.

English language arts teachers, of course, use process writing many times a week, and social science and science teachers might do so as well. The point in the illustrations given here is to demonstrate how writing process is necessary for any teacher in any subject, even those not traditionally associated with writing. For math teachers, for example, the standards published by the National Council for Teachers of Mathematics (NCTM, 2003) describe uses of writing processes to clarify math logic and understanding of qualification skills.

The National Council for Teachers of English (2003) Co-learn Web site (http://www.ncte.org/profdev/online/colearnwi/116652.htm) provides an excellent resource on the Web for teachers to equip themselves better in the teaching of writing. Materials there can help teachers of writing to see themselves as writers, look at their processes for teaching writing, and understand how writing works by looking at their students as writers. Yet another excellent resource for all teachers can be found on the NCTE Web site "Read, Write, Think," a page mutually sponsored by NCTE and the International Reading Association (http://www.readwritethink.org/). As of August 2004, this site contained actual lessons, standards, other Web resources, and student materials.

Yet another writing teacher resource is "The ABC's of the Writing Process: A Universal Process for Any Writing Task" (http://www.angelfire.com/wi/writingprocess/). This public grant-supported Web site offers teachers lesson materials, writer-workshop training, and guides in the use of process writing, which expands on the information provided in this chapter.

SUMMARY

The teaching of writing is the responsibility of all teachers, not simply the teacher of English language arts. Writing is communication, and all subjects require communication. Thus, it is imperative that all teachers understand and use the writing process as a tool to help students communicate. Certain types of writing may be applicable to particular disciplines; therefore, teachers of discipline-based classes will want to select those types that are most useful.

The contents of this chapter are designed to assist all teachers and instructional supervisors as they integrate the writing process within content areas. More exhaustive references on process writing are available, and these are listed in the References, should the reader seek deeper and more thorough analyses of the writing process.

9

Teaching Children
With Special Needs

Guiding Questions

1. Effective teaching means that all children learn. How can a teacher ensure that special needs youngsters are well served in the classroom?
2. What does the law say about children in your class who have recognized handicaps?
3. What special strategies are known to be effective with special needs learners? Are these truly limited to this population, or do they have a role to play with all learners?
4. What happens when special needs learners are mainstreamed? Is it a good thing or a bad thing? Why?
5. What is an English language learner, and how will effective teachers prepare to serve them?
6. What is pupil-centered teaching? Who should do it? For whom should it be done? Why?

Student teachers and new teachers often plead for help when asked to teach a class where many youngsters with very special learning needs have been placed. Youngsters with learning disabilities, emotionally disturbed students, and learners whose first language is not English—*all* are commonly found in large numbers in classrooms taught by the least experienced teachers. The standards for teaching (see Chapter 1) emphasize that effective teachers will teach *all* the students—that each and every student, regardless of personal characteristics, will be helped to achieve the maximum possible education. In this chapter, we offer some suggestions aimed specifically at helping inexperienced teachers to cope with the demands placed on instruction by serving students with specialized needs.

In truth, these strategies are not really different from other strategies and methods suggested throughout this book. Teaching students with specialized needs requires no unique methodology—merely *effective teaching.* Effective teachers never teach the whole class but rather teach to diverse needs within the class. Effective teachers always understand the desired learning outcomes of each learning experience. They prepare to deliver the experience so that every pupil can make individually meaningful connections. Effective teaching requires that learners demonstrate success and that teachers pursue the process until success is achieved. Effective teaching does not quit, give up, or relinquish its learners to ignorance because additional work is needed. Effective teaching accepts nothing less than demonstrated effective learning from each and every student.

LEGAL BACKGROUND FOR SPECIAL EDUCATION

For several decades, teachers across America have been required to serve students with disabilities according to provisions of federal law—the Individuals with Disabilities Education Act (P.L. 94–142). Every student with disabilities must be provided with a "free appropriate public education." The provisions of law and policy have evolved over the years, but there are some common issues to which all schools and teachers must attend (Colachico, 1996).

Least Restrictive Environment

The policies generally require that all students are educated in an environment where they can be most successful (usually the regular classroom), regardless of handicapping condition. Services for learners with disabilities are to become progressively less restrictive. These students are guaranteed mobility between programs. All special needs students must be reviewed every 12 months to ensure appropriate placement. A team of professionals plans the learner's program and assists the classroom teacher in providing services. Teachers, especially inexperienced ones, can expect, request, and even demand assistance from this professional team in planning for the individual needs of learners with disabilities (Colachico, 1996).

Due Process and Individualized Written Plans

A written educational plan should be developed for each special needs student according to the assessed needs and input from parents or guardians, classroom teachers, and other education professionals. This plan, the Individualized Education Program (IEP), is reviewed and revised yearly.

All planning efforts must include the parents, and a prior notice of intent to change educational placement or program must be provided to them in a timely manner. Hearings are also conducted in a timely manner and must be impartial; these criteria also apply to the ensuing appeal processes available to the student and his or her parents. Discipline must also be addressed in the IEP because certain disciplinary actions are applicable only if the student's behavior is shown not to be a direct result of the particular learner's handicapping condition.

Testing and evaluation instruments or strategies used to determine students' learning needs must avoid racial or cultural bias. Assessment reports must be made in the student's primary language by appropriately certified personnel.

Law guarantees confidentiality for these students. Plans, assessments, and any other records are not public knowledge and may not be openly discussed by teachers or other members of the school team without the parents' prior consent unless each person in the discussion is directly and presently involved in teaching the student.

MAINSTREAMED STUDENTS WITH LEARNING DISABILITIES

The most common misunderstanding about students identified as having particular learning handicaps is that they are not as "smart" as other learners. Yet, a student recognized to have a visual impairment would not be presumed to be unintelligent. A student paralyzed from the neck down would not be treated as dumb. Nevertheless, an insistence that youngsters with learning disabilities should be treated as "slow learners" led to placing them in special classes.

Since 1985, efforts have been under way to change this thinking among teachers and the community at large. One such effort is often referred to as *mainstreaming*—placing students with disabilities into regular classes to interact with grade-level populations for instruction deemed appropriate by the student study team. In some states, recent laws require that special needs students be included in regular classroom environments whenever possible. Without debating the merit of such a policy, we conclude that it is important to assist teachers with skills that will prove useful for these assignments.

Some general teaching tips assist teachers who must serve students with disabilities along with the diverse needs of other learners. As discussed earlier, these techniques are not really new or unique among "good" teachers but are merely a teacher's efforts to reach the learner. Teachers who teach individuals within their classes rather than the whole class use these strategies naturally. But in some schools, the culture has conditioned us to expect learners to, in a sense, meet the needs of the teacher. In such an environment, the burden of extra effort and the blame for student failure may be placed wholly on the student. This inverse view of effective teaching is most disconcerting to a learner who is also battling one or more handicapping conditions.

ENGLISH LANGUAGE LEARNERS

Who among us has never ventured into a foreign country, or at least into a room filled with native speakers of a language other than English? If we are not proficient in that other language, how lost do we feel? There is that emptiness in the pit of our stomach. People seem to be looking at us, speaking sounds, smiling, frowning, and raising their voice volume to better communicate their thoughts, but, to use a common phrase, to us it is all Greek (presuming we don't speak that language either). Fear may even be present in us when we are surrounded by people speaking something that we just can't understand. Such is the challenge to the English Language Learner (ELL).

One important consideration is to involve at least some of the student's native language in the learning process. Many studies claim to support one of several approaches to bilingual education, although this has become so terribly politicized that discussing it is a difficult challenge. In a 1998 meta-investigation, however, it was reported that when students were taught in ways that involve some of their native language, their performance was noticeably improved when measured by English language standardized tests. They outperformed other ELL students who had been taught using only English (Greene, 1998). One caveat from this study and others is that the students who benefited were already literate in their native language. Many challenges to this research continue, but for political ends. The teacher, however, can address ELL students' needs well if, when designing methods, elements of the students' native language are connected. Usually, the teacher will not be fluent in such languages, and in some school communities, there are so many non-English-language groups that no teacher could be found who could speak them all.

There are several well-researched methods for second-language teaching and learning that do not require the teacher to be a speaker of the student's language. All of these methods involve levels of language acquisition, with highly pictorial material and intensive vocabulary development. In fact, in some studies, students in these programs do better than students in programs where the teachers are not fully qualified as teachers, even though they are native speakers of the child's language (Cummins, 2001). Indeed, as Stephen Krashen (2000) has observed, students who are delayed too long in the acquisition of English reading fluency may miss a critical period of development during which spelling concepts can be most easily acquired. These best approaches are not at all dissimilar from the approaches suggested below for other special needs youngsters, although caution is urged against lumping ELL students together with students who have learning disabilities just for ease and simplicity. This is never a matter in which simple solutions should be sought. Parents want their children to learn English and subjects such as reading and other language arts and mathematics at the same academic level as all other students.

The U.S. Department of Education (2004) has codified and published expectations that require schools to provide ELL students with the same types and qualities of educational experiences—those that meet the same high academic standards that are set for native English-speaking learners. No specific method for teaching with ELL students is mandated by the No Child Left Behind Act, only that ELL students receive equitable quality instruction.

The important thing is to teach the whole child. In doing this, one can never ignore the child's culture and native language. So much in conceptual learning is tied to language that care must be taken to connect English-language culture concepts to parallel ones in native-language culture wherever possible. Ignoring such cultural connections smacks of what Lindsey et al. (2003) calls techniques similar to those used by Nazis in pre-World War II Germany in efforts to eradicate Jewish heritage and memory from society.

STUDENT-CENTERED TEACHING TIPS

Our first reminder is to begin the lesson by giving students a reason to be motivated. Be sure to relate to previous understanding and to cause students to make a connection between the earlier and the new learning. Provide a lesson objective in such terms that students will understand what to expect in their own learning. Such objectives must be short-term and observable (see earlier chapter on educational objectives).

Materials used as examples should be—as much as possible—familiar to students. Simulations and games are often effective (see several of the models discussed earlier for ideas and examples). Be sure to give concrete, specific feedback, and suggest elements that will lead to improvement. Check with students to see that they understand the suggestions and the next elements in the learning process (Colachico, 1996).

Time is an important issue. Few things in life are time tested. Yet in school, we place a high value on timed responses. Remembering that learners with disabilities must combat other distractions, consciously reorient their thinking processes, and substitute strategies to overcome their handicapping condition, we must be sure to remove the barrier of time testing. Give them the time they need to negotiate the activity. You would not require a quadriplegic to complete a quarter-mile lap around the track as quickly as a typical runner. Why, then, make such an obstacle for a learner who must consciously reorient the visual images on a written page to decode and make sense of the content?

Leaders in the field of education for special needs youngsters suggest the following strategies. There are no miracle methods for such students, only good teaching strategies that make individual assessment and diagnosis a key part of any learning plan. The general teaching strategies listed below exemplify strong teaching and will enhance learning in any students, regardless of their functioning level. Included thereafter are discipline-specific strategies to consider when teaching students with special needs.

Vocabulary Strategies

- Define words as simply as possible
- Use operational definitions, that is, explain what *it* is used for; also test vocabulary on this basis

- Deal with new vocabulary terms by relating them to previously learned words and concepts
- Have students explain vocabulary in their own words
- If applicable, show the language root of a word, for example, pyrometer comes from *pyro* (meaning fire) and *meter* (meaning measuring device).

Environmental Strategies

- Provide preferential seating near the front of the room
- Provide a study carrel
- Arrange a special pupil's seating near a student who can assist with assignments
- If necessary, consider a change of classroom
- Keep the student's desk free of extraneous material
- Allow work to be done in a quiet area

Organizational Strategies

- Set clear time limits for assignments
- Limit assignments to essential material
- Require that assignments be written down and kept in a notebook according to subject
- Allow additional time to complete a task or test
- Ask the student to paraphrase directions for an assignment in his or her own words
- Follow a daily routine; let students know ahead of time when a routine will change

Motivational Strategies

- Check papers by showing a *C* for correct items
- Give immediate reinforcement for a correct response
- Set a daily or weekly goal with the pupil
- Help students keep graphs or charts of daily and weekly progress
- Set up a simple home-to-school communication system about student progress

Presentation Strategies

- Give assignments both orally and in writing
- Change activities to accommodate short attention spans
- Give directions and information in small units
- Use simplified worksheets, especially in math
- Use concrete and manipulative objects
- Highlight key textbook passages; use markers to indicate where an assignment starts and stops
- Provide specific questions to guide students' reading

- Tape lessons so students can listen to them again
- Allow students to have sample or practice tests

Curriculum Strategies

- Provide similar materials to reinforce the concept being studied
- Provide a study guide
- Reduce the required mastery of material to key concepts
- Provide opportunities for extra drill and practice
- Use peer tutors

Reading

- Simplify and/or clarify the levels of language used in print materials
- Make the work more concrete by using manipulatives, pictures, and so on
- Reduce the number of new ideas
- Relate to previous experience or something the student already knows
- Set a focus with questions designed to guide the pupil through the material to be read
- Provide alternate media such as computer, video, and so on
- Create an additional input source by putting the text on tape (auditory to complement visual)
- Pre-teach; tell the students what they will learn
- Use "cloze" (a fill-in-the-blank) instructional technique

Mathematics

Learning in mathematics relies heavily on reading skills. Teachers can significantly assist students with disabilities to help them apply special reading and study skills to mathematics learning tasks. Students should be assisted to

- Read material for main ideas
- Read for organization, perhaps listing in one column the points given and in the second column the points needed
- Translate verbal symbols into mathematical symbols and formulas
- Read for relationships and translate these into an equation
- Follow a definite procedure that includes learning the meanings of all words, understanding what the problem asks, identifying the facts needed to discover a solution, deciding which mathematical processes are required, and identifying the order of problem-solving elements
- Make a drawing of the problem
- Study the contrast between the way words are used in math and in other areas
- Learn the proper symbols and abbreviations

Science

Reading in science requires the ability to follow a sequence of events. Directions are a very important factor. Reading in science is usually careful, analytical, and slow. Some of the terms are mathematical in nature. Some common words are used in a special sense (e.g., *force, body*). Statements are concise. Teachers can help students by doing the following:

- Simplify the vocabulary; students may need to be taught how to understand technical symbols, graphs, maps, charts, diagrams, formulas, scales, and equations
- Have students read for main ideas: "The purpose of this experiment is . . ."
- Require students to organize the material, write down the elements in an experiment, and so on
- Use videos and computer media to illustrate and develop concepts
- Assist students to adjust reading speed to the difficulty level of the material, the purposes for the reading, and the pupil's own familiarity with it
- Teach students to use the problem-solving technique: formulation of hypothesis, collation, evaluation, and organization of observed evidence, forming a conclusion and testing the conclusion
- Teach students to recognize a sequence of elements
- Conduct "hunts" for information using bibliographies, encyclopedias, library catalogs, computer and online database files, and so on
- Direct students in developing summaries and outlines

Social Studies

Social studies, like the other content domains of learning, requires reading as a primary input device so that the pupil might make connections among social relationships, concepts, and issues. Students are called on to understand new and unfamiliar vocabulary. They need to learn how to interpret information from maps, charts, diagrams, and graphs. They must know how to read critically, not accepting everything they read as true and unchallengeable. They must understand the difference between opinion and fact as they interpret written material about social issues and concepts. To assist a student with learning disabilities, one must begin with the social studies materials. The teacher must know what specific skills to teach and the methods by which each will best be delivered.

- Call attention to new words, duplicate them for the pupil, use them in appropriate context, and require students to use them
- Use films, charts, and so on to illustrate new concepts
- Require that students read for specific purposes: to answer a question, to identify the cause, to outline, and so on
- Provide numerous activities to stimulate critical thinking and analysis, assisting students to break down complex information and then to reassemble it in new ways, evaluating their ideas
- Constantly evaluate students' proficiency in reading social studies materials
- Make assignments specific enough so the pupil will know how to read; for example, a teacher may require a pupil to identify the author's point of view

Listed below are strategies that complement individual learning styles: auditory, visual, and kinesthetic.

Auditory Learner Strategies

- Give oral as well as written directions
- Tape important reading material for students to listen to as they read a passage
- Put assignment directions on tape so students can replay them when needed
- Give students oral rather than written tests
- Have students read or drill essential information with a tape recorder, reciting information into the recorder and playing it back
- Use published audiotapes with students
- Have students read or drill aloud to themselves or with another pupil
- Have another pupil read important information to students with learning disabilities
- Have students repeat words aloud while writing them down on paper in order to keep them from leaving out words or phrases
- Have students silently vocalize material mentally
- Have learners close their eyes and try to "hear" words or information, repeating in order to block out distractions
- Use a phonics approach

Visual Learner Strategies

- Use flash cards
- Have students attempt to visualize words or information with eyes closed (to minimize distractions)
- Ask students to write memos and notes to themselves concerning important words
- Write directions for assignments in clearly discernible lettering and post them
- Use videos, computers, or other media to reinforce classroom instruction
- Use the "sight word" approach to reading development

Kinesthetic Learner Strategies

- Provide clear orientations to space and location in the world
- Use charts, maps, graphs, and contrasting images
- Provide hands-on activities in all subject areas
- Make use of *appropriate* teacher touch while talking in order to get and maintain attention
- Permit learning by moving or doing
- Challenge students with role-playing, sports, drama, simulated life situations, and so on
- Reward with free exploration of manipulative or hands-on art, such as clay or sand sculpting (Colachico, 1996)

When a teacher employs techniques such as these, all learners benefit. When teachers keep their quivers filled with techniques and methods they have developed to meet certain types of special need, they can often reapply such strategies, with modification, of course, to the other youngsters with similar characteristics. It is most important that the effective teacher receive every student as he or she is and then proceed to raise each learner as high as possible in learning outcomes during the time available to make such change. Some teachers wind up with high-functioning learners, and their classes perform quite well. But *effective teachers* are effective with *all* students.

10

Student Assessment and Grading

Guiding Questions

1. How can you explain the difference between a student's grade and an assessment of a student's learning?
2. Are grades a reward/punishment or a report of progress? Might there be a difference in how grades are used with students depending on the answer to this philosophical question?
3. Describe a weighted letter-grade system.
4. What is a point system for grading, and how does it fit with school and district policies on grades?
5. How would a teacher determine a rational basis for a letter-grade weighting or a point value for a given assignment?
6. Can grades ever be truly objective or are we merely managing our subjectivity?

DEVELOP *YOUR* PERSONAL PHILOSOPHY

Effective teachers must form and establish a *personal* philosophy for grading. The most critical question is this: *Are grades to be a reward or, rather, a communication device?* Although this matter is a teacher's individual decision, communication is strongly recommended over grades as rewards. The teaching standards require that teachers be effective in determining the levels of learning outcomes achieved by students. These outcomes, like the instructional methodologies, are unique and individual, so the methods for assessing such outcomes must also be unique as well. The issues in evaluation of student learning go far beyond the simplistic and often misused process of putting a letter grade in a square on a report card.

There are many models, strategies, or methods of grading that teachers may have experienced throughout their years as students. Sometimes, teachers give grades as they were graded themselves—sometimes, as they would like to have been graded. A teacher may be surprised when asked by a parent or an administrator for reasons, or a rationale, to support his or her approach to grading. However, every teacher should consider the options and be prepared to explain strategies used in evaluating students. In particular, teachers should be ready to show how their procedures are *helpful* to students and their parents.

The following key ideas are offered as recommendations in developing a grading system or philosophy.

- Report card grades should reflect a variety of types of student performance, including classwork, homework, reports, projects, and tests. By adopting this approach, a teacher gives more students a chance to shine.

- No teacher wants to alienate or discourage students. So, one might be a little lenient at first by not expecting specific, narrow answers. By offering extra credit or bonus options in a grading system, one gives students a second chance. Keep in mind that the grade reports students' progress. As they think about grading, teachers could possibly slip, even if unintentionally, into the mode of "paying a student back."

- Competition among students of varying capabilities is often damaging to students.

- Use of a bell or normal curve for grading is *unfair* to students, and it is an *inappropriate* application of this statistical procedure. To use it makes three false assumptions: (a) that all classes are alike; (b) that every class is like a norm group of thousands of students from all parts of the country; and (c) that despite the most prodigious efforts on the part of teachers and pupils, the same number of students should fail as excel.

- Criterion-referenced tests are developed from lesson, unit, or course objectives to allow students to demonstrate mastery of required knowledge and skills. They offer the advantages of allowing students to compete only with themselves. Also, they clearly inform students what is expected of them before they take each test. They are recommended for these reasons.

- The final decision about the grade to be assigned to a student should always consider what is best for that student.

- Unlike the act of measurement, grading and evaluation cannot be performed in the absence of the teacher's own values. Reading the literature on authentic assessment, for example, one finds arguments in support of processes that require students to demonstrate learning in real-world activities. Many districts are moving to this form of assessment. Read the district's official policy on grading; *all* districts have one.

TYPES OF TESTS

Teacher-made tests take several forms, each with its strengths and weaknesses. Three major categories of tests are (a) objective, (b) short-answer, and (c) essay. First, objective tests, including fill-in-the-blank, true-false, multiple choice, and matching, are often selected for teacher convenience because they can be prepared on Scantron forms and easily graded.

Second, short-answer subjective tests, including short-answer essay questions, oral performances, and interviews, require teachers to review the answer's content and make a relatively subjective judgment as to the degree to which the answer meets expectations. Teachers often attempt to quantify essay answers by identifying in advance those key components that must be included in the answer. The answer is then read, and the key components are checked off as they are found. These are often scored on a point system.

Essay tests are the third category, one that has been criticized for its apparent lack of objectivity, as the teacher grades after subjective analysis.

If one carefully analyzes the scoring techniques used by proponents of objective testing, one realizes that assignment of point value to answers is also highly subjective. In the end, all grading is subjective. All grading, in some way, judges the worth and value of a student's work.

TRADITIONAL GRADING SYSTEMS

There are three common approaches to course grades: the 100-point system, weighted grades based on time, and letter grades.

100-Point System

The 100-point system is the simplest. A teacher arranges assignments and tests in multiples of 4-point units, with a maximum total of 100 points. Final grades are then based on a standard of 60–69 = D; 70–79 = C; 80–89 = B; 90–100 = A.

A second version of this, the 1,000-point scale, is essentially this scale multiplied by 10. It permits giving final-grade points for every daily assignment and many activities. It also allows special bonus points that serve as rewards but do not change the grade appreciably.

Weighting by Time

Another approach is to weight grades according to the time invested. Figure 10.1 illustrates a teacher's plan to determine the worth of assignments

Figure 10.1 Example of Weighting Grades by Time Required in One Grading
Period

Activity	Estimate of Time Required	Percent[a]
Homework 30×40 minutes	20 hours	40%
Class work 20×30 minutes	10 hours	20%
Group project	6 hours	12%
Weekly tests 6×50 minutes	5 hours	10%
Term paper	4 hours	8%
Oral presentation of project	3 hours	6%
Final exam	1 hour	2%
Total	49 hours (50)	98% (100%)

Source: adapted from Henson (1993)

Note: Because the total comes to 98%, a teacher might adjust by adding 2% to a more important assignment—or by subtracting lost points from 100, rather than adding points gained to zero.

a. 2% of the total grade for each hour spent

based on a ratio of the time each requires for completion to a total of 50 hours of class meeting time. If a teacher does not agree with these weights, they may be adjusted to his or her preference.

Standard Letter Grades

Another common method of grading is to assign a letter grade to each and every assignment and then to average these letter grades at the end of the grading period. Certain assignments, such as term papers and section tests or the final exam, may be multiply weighted. For example, an A is worth 4 points, but the final exam might be five-weighted and so is worth the same as five normal assignments: AAAAA = 20 grade points (on a 4.0 scale).

At the end of the grading period, the teacher totals up the grade units and divides by the number of unit entries. For example, 45 regular assignments + 3 five-weighted assignments + 1 ten-weighted assignment = 70 grade units. One adds up the As, Bs, Cs, and Ds on a 4-point grade scale (A = 4 points, B = 3 points, etc.) and allows + 0.4 for a + notation and − 0.2 for a − notation. Add all these decimal figures and divide by 70 for the term average (pretty complicated, huh?).

AUTHENTIC ASSESSMENT

Throughout its three-decade existence, authentic assessment has been alternately promoted as the more appropriate way to evaluate and report student achievement and then denigrated as irrelevant to real learning assessment. Controversy and disagreement surround systematic use of this method as a total replacement for more traditional formats for student assessment. High-stakes testing proponents such as those who abound in national policy agencies and state education departments cling to the standardized test score like drowning people to a life preserver. Policymakers inundate school staffs with criterion-referenced and norm-referenced tests that are supposed to give a score demonstrating how Johnny in Birmingham, Alabama, is doing in his fourth-grade math, compared to Juan, in Anaheim, California, and both contrasted with Ling Su in Seattle, Washington.

Grant Wiggins, nationally noted expert on curriculum design and learning assessment, has pointed out that national policy organizations and legal authorities for educational planning are not best equipped to undertake assessment in any way that approaches authenticity. They have to assess millions of learners' outcomes and do it in the most cost-effective manner, obtaining representative data that are easiest for their constituents to understand. But this does not hold up for local districts, according to Wiggins. If teachers are well-trained in making careful assessments with common rubrics or measures of quality, then there are built-in systems for real authentic assessment in local schools that are not generally available to state and national agencies (Wiggins, 2002).

One major conflict arises from a difference of philosophy about grades: whether they are a report of student progress or a surrogate payoff. Teachers have sometimes used grades as threats and rewards, seeking to punish or reinforce student behavior. At the same time, some of the same teachers then expect and encourage students to seek maximum learning, attempting to downplay the grade and suggesting that learners ought not to pursue an A but rather should seek full knowledge and skill.

Another difficulty contributing to lack of clarity is a common misconception about objectivity in grading. Try as we will, teachers have yet to create a completely objective assessment process. All grading plans have a point at which each teacher individually imposes a value judgment that is a product of his or her accumulated training and experience. It does not take long, listening to a conversation among teachers, to discover that these valuing points are vastly different.

On one hand, the debate is not resolved by research; few research reports have investigated validity or desirability of authentic assessment. On the other hand, research at the Center for Research on Evaluation Standards and Student Testing (CRESST) does verify that letter grades fail consistently to give parents and students insight into helping students improve. Teachers are most inconsistent at determining the break points between grades. All teachers have an *individual* "benefit of the doubt" philosophy that defies categorization.

In support of authentic assessment, students are said to have demonstrated improved accomplishment in schools where interrater reliability has been verified in an authentic scoring process. The improvement has broken down, however, when compared with standardized (norm-referenced) test data. Students whose improvement is demonstrated on the authentic measure do not necessarily also demonstrate improvement on the standardized test. Still, authentic assessment teachers can take comfort in the reality that even in the so-called standardized tests, it is a *subjective* interpretation of information that establishes the rating or assessment of student achievement.

Although many districts have a policy that standardizes grades (for instance, 60 = D, 70 = C, 80 = B, and 90 = A), and the numbers represent a percentage of possible accomplishment points or credits, teachers remain largely inconsistent in the process of quantifying coursework into percentage points. To disguise this arbitrariness, teachers create complex grading systems. What distinguishes a low A from a high B? Ask 50 teachers, and you may get 50 divergent views. Add to this the complexity of boiling down the many-faceted student performance picture to one simple symbol. More sleight of hand than fair assessment, this leads to inauthentic relationships between teachers and students.

Proponents of a more authentic way of assessing student progress have been encouraging teachers to reflect on students' accomplishments in real-world products, rather than representative categories. Authentic assessment asks teachers to call on students to perform life-skills tasks that various curriculum components have been preparing them to do. Instead of tests, students create projects. They write, give speeches, develop video reports, publish materials, or solve complex problems drawn from a life-skills pool that integrates the several disciplines or areas of knowledge. Teachers then must assess each student's performance against standardized criteria, such as complete sentences, accurate syntax, paragraph organization, use of descriptive terms and expressions, and so on. A critique of this approach argues that such criteria are inconsistent from teacher to teacher. To address such critiques, some states have attempted to standardize authentic assessment criteria and explain the system to local teachers. State or district officials may put extensive effort and expense into preparing teachers with a common understanding of such criteria, only to discover in the end that many teachers interpret the information individually.

PORTFOLIO ASSESSMENT

One of several more commonly implemented reforms in student grading makes use of the portfolio. Students are asked to maintain a collection of their best work, in much the same way that a model or an artist might present a collection of "best work." Certain expectations make the portfolio concept valuable. The most important of these is that the student, in collaboration with the teacher, selects the work to be included in the portfolio. Teachers who use this approach to student assessment say they spend much time conferencing with students regarding their progress and performance indicators. Because so much subjectivity is involved, prodigious effort is necessary if a teacher is to ensure the clearest possible communication with students and parents. Communication should cover what the expected standards are and how they are applied in assessing student progress toward meeting them.

Portfolio Evaluation Process Guidelines

- The end product demonstrates that a student has engaged in self-reflection.
- The portfolio is done by the student, not to the student.
- Student and teacher collaborate on selecting the pieces for the portfolio.
- Standard scores are included only if they take on added meaning in association with the student work.
- Students are given model portfolios, as well as examples of self-reflection activities and responses.

- The portfolio must convey the student's activities: rationale, intentions, contents, standards, and judgments.
- The portfolio may serve a monitoring purpose during the year and a different purpose at the end of the year.
- A student's personal goals must be reflected in the content, along with the goals of the parents, teacher, school, and district.
- The portfolio should contain material illustrating the student's growth—for example, a series of examples of actual performances showing improvement over time, changes observed on an interest inventory, records of outside activities, or attitude measures.

If a teacher chooses to use portfolio assessment to evaluate students, he or she must realize that a portfolio is not merely a work folder. Far more intensive effort from both teacher and student is involved in assessing student progress. Teachers should realize they may never feel completely comfortable with portfolio grading because the process keeps one continuously aware of systematic subjectivity.

GRADING WITH RUBRICS

A strategy that is rapidly gaining popularity among teachers is the use of scoring rubrics to evaluate student performance. Sample rubrics for evaluating writing appear in Appendices A and B. A scoring rubric is simply a set of brief descriptors of the potential finished product, with the highest value assigned to a piece that fully or most completely satisfies the quality standards for a particular lesson. Depending on the instructional situation, a teacher may decide to require demonstration only of initial understanding for a high score, or if instruction is designed for mastery, a rubric might give the top rating only to representations that are excellent in both content and mechanics.

Elements for Designing a Basic Rubric

- Identify the specifications of the intended outcome, process, product, or performance; the teacher must ask, "What exactly do I want students to do at the conclusion of the teaching?"
- Identify desired student performance levels given the desired specifications; the teacher asks, "At what level of excellence do I anticipate students will perform?"
- Identify mistakes that students should avoid—and those characteristics that are unacceptable. Ask, "What mistakes do I think, according to past experience, students might easily make?" The answer becomes a description of unacceptable work.
- Identify what is acceptable but not necessarily exemplary; this becomes the description of middle-range performance.

These elements require that a teacher have an idea as to how he or she might bring about the targeted learning behaviors. This is not a simple, linear approach. Rather, careful thought must be given to fusing student performance with context and content. The most common rubric designs are checklists of characteristics, levels-of-use descriptors, and input/output charts. Rubric design is controlled by the intended purpose or application. Another common use of rubrics can be seen in personnel evaluation systems that use behaviorally anchored rating or assessment scales.

Should rubrics be used for all types of instructional assignments? Certainly not! Rubrics should be used only when they facilitate the instructional process, when the teacher does not want evaluation of the work to become the central goal for the students. In particular, some assignments must be evaluated for summative purposes. Rubrics, however, are not best applied to this final assessment. Rather, they are most appropriate when evaluation is merely a formative process on the way to another product. Think about an assignment that is a part of an upcoming lesson. Follow the four elements described above, and brainstorm ideas for a scoring rubric for that assignment.

Rubrics are an effective, creative, and powerful tool in teaching and enhancing student learning outcomes. There are many good resources on how to produce effective rubrics. One of the more excellent, Arter and McTighe's (2000), provides a truly practical guide to teachers wanting to assess student learning more accurately and effectively. A key for success is consistency in judging students' performances. Related to this is the side benefit of helping students to learn ways of assessing the quality of their own work, introducing critical thinking strategies into their learning mix. Teachers can accomplish this with research projects or through cooperative group inquiry activities that get at real-world information. The rubrics suggested by Arter and McTighe give examples of how you can build power rubrics. Power rubrics will clarify the desired outcomes of learning, especially for those problems that are muddy and hard to define. They will lead to assessment of student-learning outcomes that are reliable.

Some key considerations when developing rubrics are worth reviewing here. First, a clear and careful alignment is required between the task skills and the curricular goals or desired outcomes. One could build a list of tasks or skills and then map them back into the outcomes. If such relationships cannot be clearly mapped, then they should not be included in the rubric.

Second, the criteria in the rubric must be observable. Teachers are producing change, and change is to be observed in products or improved skills or abilities. Internal processes cannot be evaluated unless there is an external display representing them. I cannot see *love* but only the expression and actions characteristic of love. I cannot see *thoughtfulness* but merely actions that seem to be thoughtful. Criteria in a scoring rubric must focus on the outward display of skills, abilities, and other products or performances.

Third, the language of the rubric has to be clear and specific, using vocabulary that students can reasonably be expected to understand. When you use rubrics, you give students clear descriptions of what they are expected to accomplish and the criteria by which their work is to be assessed. If the rubric is too complicated, complex, or obtuse in language, all benefit to them is lost.

Fourth, the number of points used in the rubric should reflect the value of the activity or assignment to the overall course objectives. If there is to be divergent weighting within the rubric, this should make sense to the student.

Fifth, students should not be confused about why an assignment is rated at one or another of the levels. The qualities of each level must be clear, distinct, and identifiable. Distinctions that are too fine may cause inconsistency in the scoring. The fewer the categories one uses, the clearer the rubrics are.

Finally—and this is nearly impossible to achieve, but must nevertheless be pursued—the expressions of criteria should be fair; they should be free from personal biases of the teacher. We shouldn't be asking students to perform a task in a particular way just because that is the way the teacher wants it. There should be logical rationale supporting these criteria. The criteria should not give advantage to any particular group in the class either. Students must be free to access the maximum quality (Moskal, 2003).

Back to the Taxonomies of Outcomes

Generations of children have been educated in public and private school classrooms governed by an early 20th-century idea regarding learning outcomes. Benjamin Bloom is, arguably, the most oft-quoted educational theorist in the field when it comes to building instruction plans. Over the decades, scores of teams of educational theorists have conspired to reform and modify Bloom's three basic taxonomies, especially the cognitive taxonomy, but without much success. One 21st-century theorist, Robert Marzano (2001), has reviewed Bloom's taxonomies and tweaked them into a revised perspective involving what he calls *systems thinking*. As a teacher, you can help to form *habits of the mind* in students. The process starts with the attitudes and perceptions held by learners. Next, they are to acquire and integrate new information with existing knowledge. After extending and refining this new knowledge, they are given opportunities to use it in meaningful ways. They thus apply and formulate new systems of thinking. In Marzano's revision of Bloom's taxonomy, the highest level is *creation*. This involves the generation of new ideas, products, or ways of viewing things. It could be designing, construction, planning, producing, or inventing new things. This top level scaffolds on *evaluation*, which is the justifying of decisions and courses of action, checking hypotheses, or critiquing and experimenting to determine outcomes. Prior to this, the student must be analyzing information learned and problems at hand. Comparisons, organizational patterns, deconstruction, and inquiry characterize this level. Just beneath, of course, we must find *application*. Herein students use information they are beginning to grasp from a familiar situation and carry out a task, possibly making transfer of learning into unfamiliar areas. Like Bloom, Marzano builds these all on understanding, which arises out of remembering or recalling.

Using such a taxonomy, one can build rubrics in which each level reflects differing taxonomic accomplishments. But in the end, whether we use Marzano's rubric or stick with the tried and true provided by Bloom (knowledge, understanding, application, analysis, synthesis, and evaluation), both will serve the purpose well for rubric design.

Figure 10.2 Marzano's Idea of Systems Thinking

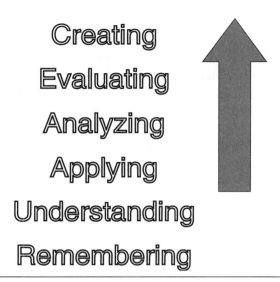

Creating

Evaluating

Analyzing

Applying

Understanding

Remembering

Sample Grading Policy 1: Kentucky

One private school, Mercy Academy, has posted the following grading policy on its Web site, http://mercy.ky.schoolwebpages.com/education/dept/deptinfo.php?sectiondetailid=472

Mercy's Grading Policy: 1.5 Grading Scale

The purposes of assessment or grading are to establish, recognize, and report the level of student achievement. Levels of achievement are established through the school grading scale in quantitative terms and by performance criteria in qualitative terms. All teachers in all courses use the following quantitative grading scale.

A+	98–100
A	94–97
A–	90–93
B+	88–89
B	85–87
B–	83–84
C+	81–82
C	78–80
C–	76–77
D+	74–75
D	72–73
D–	70–71
F	69–0

In qualitative terms, letter grades are to reflect, in general, the levels of achievement as described by the criteria below:

A High competency. Goes beyond the attainment of essential goals and objectives. Self-direction, critical thinking, and initiative clearly demonstrated.

B Thorough competency. Goes beyond the attainment of essential goals and objectives. Evidence of self-direction and critical thinking.

C Satisfactory competency. Consistent attainment of essential goals and objectives. Normal or average need for teacher direction and assistance.

D The first level of competency. Attainment of essential goals and objectives. May depend heavily on teacher direction and assistance and may reflect a student's best effort commensurate with an objectively established and verified ability range in a specific area.

Summary grades, issued at the ends of grading periods, are based on a variety of factors, including but not limited to homework, quizzes, tests, and assignments.

SOURCE: © 2001–2004 Mercy Academy > For Parents Only. All Rights Reserved (used by permission)

Sample Grading Policy 2: New Jersey

Beth Serafini (2000), of the Jersey Shore Area School District, reports their grading policy on her Web site (http://www.jsasd.k12.pa.us/bserafini/Grading%20Policy.htm) to be as follows.

Grading Policy

The Jersey Shore Area School District uses a letter grade system in the following manner:

Kindergarten

M   most of the time (satisfactory)
P   part of the time (needs to improve)
N   not yet

Primary/Intermediate—major subjects are graded by achievement. Achievement grades are grades that base student progress to that of other children on the same grade level:

A+   99–100
A   96–98
A–   94–95
B+   92–93

B	88–91
B–	86–87
C+	84–85
C	80–83
C–	78–79
D+	76–77
D	72–75
D–	70–71
F	69 and below

To get a percentage, you divide the number correct by the total number of questions. Examples:

19 correct divided by 20 total possible gives you a 95%.
14 correct divided by 15 total possible gives you a 93%.
10 correct divided by 12 total possible gives you 83%.
6 correct divided by 8 total possible gives you 75%.

Progress grades are used to inform parents how children are doing on material such as writing, art, music, physical education, social development, and work habits.

O	Outstanding
S	Satisfactory
I	Improving
N	Needs improvement
X	Comment enclosed

Sample Grading Policy 3: New York

A detailed analysis and explanation of a school district grading policy—the Guilderland Central School District of Guilderland, New York—can be found on the Web at http://www.guilderlandschools.org/district/General_Info/Grading.htm. The policy is based on the work of Thomas Guskey (2003) of the University of Kentucky. This policy provides detailed guidelines for elementary grading, middle school grading, and high school grading processes and is a good example of what school districts should address when thinking through the student evaluation activities that teachers must do several times each year.

Sample Grading Policy 4: South Carolina

The Charleston County School District in South Carolina has posted a more traditional grading policy, rating percentile ranks:

A	93–100
B	85–92
C	77–84
D	70–76
F	69 or below

For the complete grading policy, visit the district Web site at http://www.charleston.k12.sc.us/index

In such a system as this, the numerical value can be the result either of weighted grades converted from grade points to percentages or of a 100-point system of assignment values set up by the teacher. The policy gives several examples and explains the means by which grades and grade point averages are to be calculated. It serves as a good model for schools wishing to follow a more traditional grading system.

Sample Grading Policy 5: Ohio

The Marlington public school district of Alliance, Ohio, has posted a good example of a grading policy on its Web site (http://dukes.stark.k12.oh.us/grade.html). It includes this important statement of philosophy about grading in Marlington schools.

Philosophy

The Marlington Local School District believes that the process of evaluation should be continuous and assist the teacher in developing insight into the student's skill levels, achievements, attitudes, interests, and personal growth and development.

It is essential that a pupil be evaluated in terms of his or her skills and achievements in relation to the achievement of others in his or her class. However, it is recognized that all pupils are individuals and learn at different rates. The expertise of the teacher enables a careful blending of this subjective and objective information in determining the best evaluation of the child.

Evaluation information should be effectively communicated so that parents and pupils understand the achievement level of the child.

Some of the standards used to determine the level of achievement include: graded course of study, state academic content standards, completion of assigned projects and/or daily work, achievement tests, classroom participation, attendance, and ability to listen and follow directions.

Grades are a consequence of learning and not the purpose of learning.

SUMMARY

Assessment and grading are thorny issues for a professional educator. They raise issues of objectivity versus subjectivity and communication modes to students, parents, and administrators. The recent move toward authentic assessment also involves complex and unresolved issues. In the final analysis, each teacher must review intended content and existing context, assess student needs, develop instructional objectives, and match assessment procedures to the situation. It is essential, therefore, that teachers examine and carefully reflect on their grading standards, approaches, and rationale for each element or procedure they undertake when it comes to assessing student growth. Grades, to learners, are so intensely personal and so much associated with self-worth. Carelessness in grading processes could possibly even be harmful. We spoke of a golden rule standard when we discussed classroom conduct and behavior management. A similar approach is advised here as well: Grade students in ways that you, as a learner, would also want to be graded.

11

Putting It All Together for Professional Teaching

Guiding Questions

1. What is a blended model method, and how many should I own?
2. How can I blend elements of different models into my own method?
3. Why would I use elements from different models to make up my method?
4. Would I ever just use a whole model?
5. Which grade levels are best for the blended model method?
6. Which blended model elements might I already use in the lessons I typically design?

TEACHING AND LEARNING: A SCIENCE/ART FORM . . . AND ITS OUTCOME

Learners acquire knowledge in different ways, for different purposes, and at differing levels of mastery. Individual readiness is a reality that psychologists discuss, politicians and board members do not understand, and parents often forget. Nevertheless, it is a reality to which every teacher must adjust. Self-concept relates to individual perceptions about achievement, unique personality, individual ability, and present levels of cognitive development.

These are but a few of the dimensions on which learners differ. These same differences among learners affect teachers as well. Like the painter, the *teacher-artist* creates an art form by selecting just the right *color* of skill development or information applied in just the right *technique* on just the right *surface* for just the right desired *end.* He or she takes into account dynamic relationships with several students and the collective class group, the fusion of individual and collective experiences with which each class member begins class every day. The agenda must include intermediate and ultimate outcomes expected by society for these learners, as well as the individual needs that these particular students consciously and unconsciously call out to have met.

Then, the *teacher-scientist* takes over and, through a very systematic process, creates instructional content and activities that maximize student learning. With considerable understanding of the varied models and methods available and the outcome that each is likely to produce, the teacher blends ideas, activities, and instructional approaches together with content for a precisely prescribed *blended model method* lesson.

THE BLENDED MODEL METHOD: SOME SAMPLE PLANS

I recommend that teachers assess each learning situation and develop a particular teaching method to meet the needs of the situation—both the teacher's and the students' needs. Someone visiting the classrooms of *effective* teachers is not likely to see any one of the models discussed earlier in this book. More likely, the observer finds an artistically crafted, scientifically developed method that permits that particular teacher to communicate with and encourage learning among particular students with unique needs relating to a specific curriculum. Good teachers take components of models and blend them into efficient, effective personal methods. Methods that prove to be consistently effective are methods teachers remember and retain in their collection or methodology.

With the permission of their originators, I have included some highly creative samples of blended model lessons crafted by excellent young teachers who had received systematic instruction in the various models. They are not offered for immediate application, for each teacher constructed the method to meet his or her specific needs. Rather, these sample lessons are included in this book to illustrate how creative teachers can draw from the models to develop very clever methodology. Each reader can do the same.

Sample Blended Model Method
Lesson 1: Classroom Management—Setting the Tone

Stacey Tisor developed the following blended model method lesson for the first day of school, setting the tone for the term. This method draws from concept construction, direct instruction, cooperative inquiry, and teams-games-tournaments cooperative learning.

Objective: Students will decide that the teacher is to be in charge of the class and will understand course requirements and personal responsibilities in the course.

Procedure

1. The teacher introduces herself and explains what the class is about. Course objectives are presented for discussion. The teacher's grading policy is explained.

2. The teacher divides the class into groups of four students each. Groups are asked to come up with four rules for the classroom this term.

3. The teacher has each group report its four rules and the rationale for each. The possible rules are listed on the board. The rules are consolidated into four class rules that all can "own."

4. The teacher now distributes her management plan, which contains the rules she had anticipated for the class. The discrepancies are discussed so that the class sees that *all* are in agreement over the rules for the year. The rest of the management plan is explained, illustrated, and probed by the teacher.

5. The teacher asks students to write on a card what they expect from her during the term. These cards are discussed, and she commits to pursuing all those that are realistic and possible.

6. Students, back in their cooperative groups, play a quiz game regarding the class rules and the management procedures.

Sample Blended Model Method Lesson 2:
History—Involvement in Foreign Conflicts

Roger Hsu created the following blended model lesson incorporating components from concept construction, cooperative learning, Socratic inquiry, and peer practice for his urban high school students.

Objective: Students will be able to identify historical features and form opinions on the issue of U.S. involvement in foreign conflicts.

Element 1: Introduction

The anticipatory set question is written on the overhead for all students to see: "You are witness to a friend being pushed and socked by another kid. There is no one around to stop the assault. Would you do something—or walk away?"

Element 2: New Material

Reading material is distributed that accurately summarizes the following conflicts: World War II, Korean Police Action, the Vietnam War, and the Gulf War. Another set of materials distributed summarizes potential conflicts such as in Haiti, Cuba, former Yugoslavia, and Tibet. In addition, a series of short videos on each place is shown.

Element 3: Enumeration and Listing

Students are asked to suggest significant facts they know concerning each of the *potential* conflicts. Their ideas are written on the board.

Element 4: Labeling

The name of the war or region determines grouping of the comments from Element 3.

Element 5: Peer Practice and Memorization

Students are assigned to work in pairs. The teacher explains the roles of doer and helper and the purpose of the peer practice strategy. Pairs are given worksheets containing questions and answers about the key facts just discussed, which students memorize and learn.

Element 6: Jigsaw II

- Students are organized into study teams and expert groups.
- The home teams assign members to the expert groups.
- Each expert group focuses on and masters one of four sets of reading material: Each set relates to one historical conflict and is contrasted with one potential conflict.
- Experts return to study teams and teach the comparisons of the four historical conflicts with the four current potential conflicts.

Element 7: Socratic Inquiry

Taking positions:

- The teacher asks students to express their position on each of the various potential conflicts.
- The teacher probes and encourages high-level responses of students.

Exploring and refining stances and testing assumptions:

- As students state their positions, the teacher, with the class, probes potential consequences of their decisions.

- The teacher leads students to extend their proposed positions to ultimate possible outcomes.
- As students refine their stances on particular conflicts, the teacher checks their reasoning by challenging them on other conflicts.
- The teacher identifies assumptions and challenges relevancy.

Examples:

"Why do you assume that intervention means sending ground troops rather than smart missiles and bombers?"

"Do you assume we will be able to solve our social ills and then we will suddenly intervene in the world's social problems?"

Sample Blended Model
Method Lesson 3: English Language Arts Lesson for Limited English (Spanish-speaking) First Graders

The lesson that follows is yet another example of the blended model lesson design by National Board Certified Teacher and teacher-coach Marta Gardner. Notice how she smartly blends together elements from the Hunter direct instruction model and writing process model elements as well as creative application of Socratic inquiry. The lesson was designed as a demonstration lesson teaching literacy and language arts to second-language learners in the first grade.

Objective/Outcome: Students will explain and illustrate how to give simple directions.

Content Standards: Listening and speaking; give, restate, and follow simple directions; writing: selecting a focus, penmanship, and conventions

Element 1

Review and connect to last class day's brainstorming activity about topics for writing directions (direct instruction model, anticipatory set)

Element 2

Teacher explains and models why clear directions are important. A criteria chart about "things you need and steps in order" is used to assist students in processing information (advance organizer model).

Element 3

Teacher brainstorms things needed, using the advance organizer chart, and then proposes a discussion about making a sandwich. She uses props of bread, peanut butter, knife, etc. (direct instruction model: modeling and monitoring). The teacher next probes the students about various examples of telling directions to get them to identify which ones are most accurate. She poses scenarios to challenge their responses (Socratic inquiry model).

Element 4

The teacher offers students choices of several different activities; in each case, students will develop a series of instructional steps and then explain those steps to their partner. Partners are assigned response clarification tasks (concept development model: clarification; peer practice model: responding).

Element 5

The students select a topic to write about (writing process model: prewriting; direct instruction model: guided practice; writing process model: drafting) and begin writing.

Carryover lesson to next day will include

Element 1

Students re-reading their drafts with a partner and acting out their directions (writing process model: responding; role-play model: demonstrating).

Element 2

Students will revise by adding or deleting steps and material (writing process model: editing).

Element 3

Students will clearly write their final drafts and share with class, and post on wall (writing process model: publishing).

Sample Blended Model
Method Lesson 4: Music—Development of Music Types

The following blended model method draws from concept construction, cooperative learning, and social science inquiry, with identified questioning strategies. The lesson was created by Allison Murich.

Objective: Students will analyze selected types of music and the particular historical development of each.

Key:

* = reinforcement   ^ = encouragement   # = relational probe

' = critical awareness probe   < = prompt

Element 1: Introduction (Concept Construction)

- As "What kind of music do you like to listen to?"
- As(*) "Great! Write that on the board."
- As(^) "Could you clarify that more for us?"
- As "What other kinds of music are there?"
- As(^) "Please rephrase that so we all can understand."
- As(#) "You are very close. Do you want to ask someone to assist you?"
- As(') "I think you mean '——.' Am I right?"
- As(<) "What about 'Latin Classical' as a style?"

Element 2: Looking for Relationships (Concept Construction)

The teacher has students take the various types of music listed on the board and group them by asking:

- As "How would you combine these into groups?"
- As(*) "Terrific! Go to the board and put that kind together on the left. Does everyone agree?"
- As(^) "Good! What else could be part of that group?"
- As(#) "You are really close. Can anyone help her?"
- As "What other types of music might fit into these categories?"

Element 3: Cooperative Inquiry

The teacher says: "In your groups, pick one type of music. You are going to discover the history of that particular type of music and prepare a presentation to the class." The teacher ensures that no two groups have the same topic and that all are set to function efficiently. Students use resource books and library materials to complete their research. The remainder of the class period and the next are used. After two class periods (two days), students make reports by groups.

Element 4: Presentations

- As(*) "That's very well done!"
- As(^) "Could you explain that to us more?"
- As(#) "Does anyone in your group know about '——'?"

Sample Blended Model Method Lesson 5: Abstract Art

Ed Plant provides the following sample blended model method lesson about abstract art for middle graders.

Objective: Students will identify abstract paintings as "abstract art" and develop a working understanding of the specifics of abstract art. They will then produce an abstract painting of their own, using abstraction correctly.

Element 1: Concept Construction and Writing Process

- The teacher shows slides of art works that are considered abstract art (works by Picasso, Dali, Braque, Johns, etc.). The teacher then probes and prompts students.
- "What do these paintings look like? Are there any noticeable things, objects, or people in these paintings?"
- Students are then asked to write down five thoughts that come to mind when they look at these pictures.
- The teacher or a student then writes the students' thoughts on the board.

Element 2: Concept Construction and Inquiry

The teacher probes

- "Now, can we group these thoughts or combine them in any way?"
- "Can we draw any conclusions about relationships between the pictures and the thoughts?"
- Students are asked to organize the thoughts into categories. "What could we call this one?" will be asked of each category.

The teacher then asks

- "Do these groups relate to each other?"
- "Are there any key words or phrases that will help us?"

Element 2: Concept Construction and Inquiry

The teacher next leads the class into the definition of "abstract art."

Element 3: Peer Practice and Cooperative Inquiry

Students are paired. One draws an abstract portrait of the other. One is to help the other. The students have to draw with oil pastels and chalk. The portraits must be life-size but missing at least three features. They must have colors and shapes repeating throughout the composition. When the first student is finished, the second begins.

During the process, the class is given a study guide concerning abstract art. One student quizzes the other while they draw.

Element 4: Critique and Checking
for Understanding (Direct Instruction)

A critique of these portraits is given. The teacher looks for color, shape, and abstract form and seeks to identify the subject person. A test is given on the terms, artists, and reasons surrounding abstract art.

Sample Blended Model Method Lesson 6:
Biology—Cellular Functions of Plants and Animals

Dawn Hudson, a special education science teacher in Alhambra, California, used the general teaching model format to create the following blended model method in 1993. She drew lesson components from scientific inquiry, direct instruction, peer practice, and cooperative inquiry models.

Element 1: Preparation and Planning

- Diagnose student need: Students have difficulty reading and understanding basic text information, but they are able to perform fairly well when there are graphic representations of the information and when they can physically manipulate objects.
- Construct learning objective: Students will compare the cellular functions of plants and animals.
- Consider and select tasks and activities:

    Draw examples of animal cells on the board and explain the parts

    Draw examples of plant cells and explain the parts

    Examine selected plant and animal cells under a microscope

Element 2: Framing the Lesson

- Linking to previous understanding: "On Friday we saw a video about animal and plant life. We learned that both plants and animals are made up of cells. What do you think the cells do?" Responses are discussed and probed.
- Establishing purposive focus: "Today we will read about plant and animal cells. We will find out how they are the same as, and different from, each other."
- Procedural directions: "Get into pairs. Decide who will read first and who will read second. The first person reads one paragraph out loud and explains to his or her partner what the paragraph means. The second person reads along silently, helping the partner if a mistake is made. Then, after both students are sure they understand, roles must be reversed and the next paragraph is read."

Element 3: Instructional Input and Learning

- Presentation of content: The teacher presents a mini-lecture on the same information, calling on students to fill in blanks or respond to prompts and probing questions.
- Monitoring and adjustment of understanding and of task acquisition questions.

- Throughout the mini-lecture and associated discussion the teacher attends to student responses, drawing nonresponding students in and leading low-quality responders into higher quality answers.

Element 4: Integration of the Learning for Insight and Clarification

- "How are animal and plant cells different from each other? How are they alike?"
- "Why do plants and animals grow if their cells stay about the same size?"
- "How long do cells live?"

Students move into groups to discuss the above questions and form conclusions.

Sample Blended Model Method Lesson 7:
English Language Arts: Writing Process—Peer Editing

Below is a sample blended model method lesson using components from concept construction, Socratic inquiry, direct instruction, and cooperative learning for a writing lesson in English; the lesson was created by Jeff DuBransky.

Objective: Students will

1. Generate the characteristics of good writing

2. Evaluate which characteristics are most important

3. Work in small groups to correct each other's writing

Element 1: Concept Construction (10 minutes)

- The teacher asks students: "Why are some people paid a lot of money to write stories for newspapers and magazines?"
- "What makes their writing better than others?"
- Students are asked to generate the qualities of good writing (e.g., clarity, organization, grammar, spelling).
- The teacher writes student responses on the board. After a number are listed, students are asked to group the responses into two categories: *technical* and *creative.*

Element 2: Socratic inquiry (15 minutes)

- The teacher asks each student to determine which quality is the "most important." He probes the students' responses and their reasons. Students are asked to defend their choice.

Element 3: Direct Instruction, Read-Around, Peer Editing (10 minutes)

The teacher transitions the lesson into instruction about proofreading in preparation for an upcoming assignment. Marks to use, things to look for, and so on are explained, using overhead transparencies illustrating the main ideas and correction marks. The teacher groups the students and explains how the groups are to function. Four students in the group read each of the others' papers and mark them, but within a 6-minute time frame. (This forces them to move quickly, without involving themselves in the content of the writing.)

Element 4: Cooperative Learning and
Writing Process Peer Editing (20 minutes)

Students work in groups, reading and editing each other's papers.

Element 5: Writing Process—Final Draft

Students are instructed to write final drafts of papers as homework and then turn them in the following day.

Sample Blended Model Method Lesson 8: Chemistry: Classification of Chemical Elements

Tom Christopher provides the following blended model method for a high school chemistry class studying the classification of chemical elements.

Length of Assignment: One week, five periods
Objectives:

1. Students will determine criteria (rules) used to classify the members of different groups of chemical elements. They will use these criteria to further classify new chemical elements as they are introduced.

2. Students will work in teams to analyze information and prepare to explain it to the class.

Element 1: Orientation to the Case (Socratic Inquiry)

An introduction to the objective, review of materials, and facts is given to the class. The dialectic or Socratic method is explained to the students. Students are assigned to teams.

Element 2: Identifying the Issues (Scientific
Inquiry, Cooperative Learning, Concept Construction)

Teams are given extensive lists that depict and describe the randomly enumerated elements. Each team studies the material and lists characteristics, properties, and traits for different elements selected from the handout lists. For concept construction, the group identifies possibilities for grouping the elements.

Element 3: Taking a Position (Concept Construction, Writing Process)

Students working in teams analyze, group, and regroup their elements. Each team writes out reasons (rules) for the separation criteria used to organize their representation of the elements.

Element 4: Argumentation (Socratic Inquiry, Concept Construction)

A member of each team is designated as a spokesperson to present the team's findings to the class. Each team presents its grouped elements and the rules used for grouping. The groupings are graphed. The teacher lists each team's rules on the board. Each team compares its rules with others to see if theirs are effective for the other types of representation. Each point at which a grouping of elements violates the rules is established. The rules that seem to work for most of the element groupings are accepted and listed together. The rules that do not are listed separately. The element groupings that do not seem to follow rules from all of the teams are also listed separately. Conflicts are identified and defined. Priorities are set on the rules. A hierarchy of correlation is assigned to the rules.

Element 5: Refining and Qualifying the Positions (Socratic Inquiry)

Members of each team meet to review the class's composite rule list. They analyze the separations of their team's element groups following the composite rules, looking for consistency. The rules that are universal are accepted. Any new rules the teams might discover are included in a new team rule list. Those rules that are not universal are listed separately with an explanation. Element groupings are again compared and argued. Positions are stated and defended. The class meets again and compares each team's rules for classification. The rules are qualified and accepted, then listed in a prioritized hierarchy.

*Element 6: Testing Factual Assumptions Behind
Qualified Positions (Socratic Inquiry, Concept Attainment)*

The teacher provides the class with the accepted scientific classification method and a copy of the periodic table. The teams compare their findings with the *accepted* method. They identify their factual assumptions and determine the relevance of their method as well as that of the accepted method. Each team then completes the classification exercises also provided by the teacher. Each individual is evaluated on participation, and each member receives the collective team score on the exercises.

Sample Blended Model Lesson: A Social Studies Series

The following five blended model lesson plans shown here were compiled as part of a learning unit in Grade 12 social studies, extended over a 2-week period. The lessons, which culminate in an integrated group project, are built on previous learning from social studies, local history, and geography. This integration enables students to obtain a greater understanding of and appreciation for their neighborhood environment.

Overall Objective: Students will design a city layout identifying the location, area, and size of buildings, land use areas, roads, and so on. This plan will be drawn on butcher paper as a group activity and supported by each student's contribution of a written description justifying the urbanization plan form.

Lesson 1: Setting the Scene

This blended model method lesson incorporates components from direct instruction and cooperative group learning.

Objective: Students will be introduced to the overall objective (see above) and provided with a time line and expectations for the completed project.

Element 1: Orientation

The teacher reviews previous learning and explains how students will approach this group project with research, information gathering, planning, design, and written statement. A completed design from last year's class is shown.

The teacher explains how the work content and the time frame will be spread over the next five lessons. This outline is presented:

Lesson 1: Setting the Scene

Lesson 2: Information Gathering

Lesson 3: Group Planning

Lesson 4: Group Drawing

Lesson 5: Final Design and Description

Element 2: Teaching Input

The guideline handout is distributed and read aloud line by line to check for understanding. Book resources and research information are provided. The teacher gives instruction on growth and purpose of cities, requirements of inhabitants topographical features, and transportation factors—all relative to the locality. An overhead transparency illustrates the historical growth of cities in Inland Valley, the hypothetical location of the city.

Element 3: Group Formation

The teacher assigns and arranges groups, ensuring a balanced mix. Students appoint the group leader and recorder; then information-gathering roles are given out. For example, one student is to consider highways and transportation, another to investigate shopping requirements, and so on. The teacher distributes large sheets of paper, colored pens, pencils, rulers, and other necessary materials.

Element 4: Closure

The teacher probes and questions for understanding of objectives and procedures. Emphasis is placed on students supporting one another as part of the group activity. Students are to meet in groups for the next four lessons. The grading rubric is explained; that is, assessment is based on group participation plus an individual element.

Lesson 2: Information Gathering

This blended model method lesson uses components from concept construction, concept attainment, and Socratic inquiry.

Objective: Students will gather information for analysis and evaluate land use priorities based on the arguments put forward.

Element 1: Brainstorming

The teacher asks for city land use elements. These are categorized and listed on the board under main groupings, for example, housing, shopping, offices, factories, schools, roads, parking. Relationships among groups are explored, refinements are made, and inferences are drawn.

Element 2: Essential Characteristics and Data Examples

Comparisons are made of city component groupings to determine essential characteristics of a well-balanced city. Positive and negative data examples are provided, for example, public open space versus air-polluting factories that provide jobs.

Element 3: Socratic Inquiry

Groups discuss and agree on their stance for various land uses based on views put forward. Students are encouraged to think freely and use higher-order skills to reach group consensus.

Element 4: Closure

The teacher reviews Elements 1 through 3 and checks for understanding and progress by each group. Students are to come to the next lesson prepared to begin planning their design.

Lesson 3: Group Planning

This blended model method lesson uses components from direct instruction and cooperative learning.

Objective: Students will analyze the information and material gathered and begin planning the design of their city community.

Element 1: Guided Practice

The teacher illustrates planning elements with a partially completed drawing and shows aerial block plan technique. Students are told this is not an artistic exercise; rather, the overall planning concept is more important, with demonstration of thinking through the issues.

With an overhead transparency, the teacher highlights possible problems and conflicting land use demands, for example, nonprofitable uses, provision of access roads and parking, difficulties with SLOAP (Space Left Over After Planning).

Element 2: Cooperative Learning (Jigsaw II)

Based on preassigned information-gathering roles, expert groups are formed on six different land uses:

- Housing
- Shopping and restaurants
- Offices and factories
- Roads and parking
- Social and service amenities
- Parks, sports, and recreation areas

Each expert group discusses number, size, type, and location of their specific buildings and land use. They compare and contrast their own community needs and list criteria requirements.

Students return to home study teams and relate their findings to other members. Individual expert contributions on each component enable the group to synthesize material.

Element 3: Group Practice

Groups formulate an overall plan and begin drafting the design in pencil, establishing a logical progression and interaction of urban lifestyle patterns. Directed by the leader, each student works on his or her particular sector and land use in the plan. The teacher circulates among groups to monitor progress, encourage, and answer questions.

Element 4: Closure

The teacher reviews lesson content and checks for understanding by groups.

Lesson 4: Group Drawing

This blended model method lesson is based upon elements from concept construction and cooperative groups.

Objective: Students will work in groups to draw, color, and label their city plan, justifying to one another the location of specific buildings and land uses.

Element 1: Synthesizing Information and Consolidating Insights

Students are asked to rank and defend with reasons the planning criteria for their city. Using these results, the teacher then guides students in explaining and supporting their thinking and in clarifying the rationale for their choices. The teacher demonstrates why certain cities are more attractive and successful than others in terms of living, working, and enjoyment of pleasure or recreation.

Element 2: Cooperative Groups

In their groups, students work toward completing their design layout using materials collected and referring to book and library resources for further information. The teacher checks the progress of each group.

Element 3: Closure

The teacher uses questions, prompts, and probes to ensure understanding.

Lesson 5: Design Completion

This blended model method lesson uses components from cooperative groups, concept construction, and writing process.

Objective: Students will complete the illustrated design, with title, north point, approximate scale, and labels. They will support their planning ideas with a written descriptive statement.

Element 1: Cooperative Groups

Students finalize their group activity by refining and polishing their drawing in color with annotations in ink.

Element 2: Inferences and Predictions

Guided by the group leader, students discuss and draw conclusions about the completed project. The teacher encourages critical analysis, for example:

"What are the best and worst elements of the Plan?"
"Would you do anything differently another time?"
"Would you like to live in this city?"

Element 3: Writing Process

1. Students engage in prewriting activity by stimulating a flow of ideas from outlining, mapping, and debating.

2. Students compose a draft under headings of description, justification of ideas, their own input, and learning outcomes.

3. Students share their writing in read-around groups. Final revising and editing follows, using home study time to complete if necessary.

Element 4: Closure

- The teacher is to summarize the design planning process experienced by the class.
- Each group presents its project with individual written statements pinned up on the wall. The teacher prepares students for a critical review of each other's work during the next class session.

Element 5: Extended Practice

The teacher plans to show the video *Urban City Planning* and arranges a visit to the local City Hall to see maps and models and experience the role and responsibilities of the Planning Commission.

We can see from our sample lessons that real teaching takes over at the point of the blended model application. All of the earlier patterns and models presented are nice, but the vast majority of the models and methods of teaching that you will use, *you* will create to meet the needs of specific children. Therefore, to expect to apply a canned lesson plan or even a canned lesson pattern as a usual practice will not equip you to serve each child so that *all* those in your classrooms learn well. We know full well that our standards for teaching require us to ensure learning for each and every one of those precious pupils—yes, even the obstinate and irritating ones. In our exploration of teaching as professionals, we can never expect to just throw away some of those in our charge who are less than convenient for us to teach. Our job is to find a way to teach each one. That is why they will call us *teacher*!

RECOMMENDATION FOR FURTHER STUDY IN TEACHING EXCELLENCE

As was reported in the foreword and the introduction, I am indebted to Bruce Joyce and Marcia Weil (2000), and their other co-authors, researchers, and sources. Their landmark work, *Models of Teaching*, now in its sixth edition, will probably endure throughout the foreseeable future as one of the best books of research into teaching processes and methodologies. Anyone who would become a master of teaching and a trainer of teachers must read and re-read this work.

Another excellent resource can be found in *Differentiated Instructional Strategies for Writing in the Content Areas,* by Carolyn Chapman and Rita King (2003). In this one guide, you will find specific, explicit strategies for teaching writing processes while at the same time delivering the content standards. The authors help to enable teachers to work with each student's unique skills and needs so that the student learns to apply information, to demonstrate content mastery, to think and write creatively and critically, and to solve real-world problems.

One additional suggested resource is *Teaching English Language Learners K–12: A Quick-Start Guide for the New Teacher,* by Jerry Jessness (2004). This author provides real strategies for maintaining sensitivity to students who are learning under the added handicap of needing to learn English. The sound theoretical content is easy to read and provides relevant and practical help when planning instruction for this population.

CONCLUDING THOUGHTS ON THE JOURNEY OF THE TEACHER

Direct instruction, concept construction, Socratic inquiry, writing process, classroom discipline, and all the other models discussed in this book are intended for your *creative* application. These models of learning, as stated in the beginning, are not recipes or guaranteed-successful, off-the-shelf lesson plans. Rather, they represent the most widely recognized models and strategies applied through decades by successful teachers to meet desired instructional goals and objectives. Rarely do effective teachers use a single model or strategy. Most often, these models are mixed and commingled, just as a painter mixes basic colors to create desired shades and hues. It is most important that the professional teacher and the expert instructional leader know the basic colors (the models and related strategies) and how they look when mixed and blended (methods and methodologies) to achieve different shades of understanding and application, targeted for an infinite number of different learning situations.

As *you,* the professional educator, attempt to create and transmit your art form in a manner both scientific and aesthetic, you are encouraged to draw from all these models, strategies, and methods. The ancient archer's quiver was always packed with many different types of arrows, each crafted by the archer for different purposes and situations. The education professional's quiver must also be filled with models, strategies, and *personally blended* teaching methodologies— arrows that will hit the target and meet the needs of the learners, transmitting true mastery of skills, knowledge, abilities, and insights to our growing generations of new citizens. Here's to teaching that is well prepared, well planned, well aimed, and well focused . . . always right *on target.*

Appendix A

Sample Four-Point Rubric for Holistic Scoring, Grades K–8

A four-point rubric for general scoring of papers from Grades 1 through 8, in the various types of writing, is presented only as an example, not as a model or pattern to be closely followed.

Grade 1

4 points

- The piece is well organized, is "whole," or at least sticks with a theme or focus throughout.
- The piece is interesting for some reason or other; it may be fresh, energetic, or imaginative.
- Specific details help paint a whole picture.

3 points

- The piece has some organization or some sense of wholeness, and some development of an idea, focus, or story; but a statement may be added that does not fit into the story.
- The writing is somewhat interesting or imaginative.
- Some specific details are provided.

2 points

- The paper does not have a single theme or focus and therefore may lack organization.
- However, there is something redeeming about the content or language—some slightly interesting thought or phrase, or the presence of a natural voice.

1 point

- The predominant characteristic of a "1" paper is that it lacks organization, theme, or focus; it merely answers questions posed by the scribe or the task.

Grade 2

4 points

- The story is imaginative, shows feeling, and holds the reader's interest.
- The paper is sequential in that one idea is developed before going on to the next.
- The paper is detailed and descriptive; the writer explains why and how and uses adjectives and adverbs correctly; there is variety in language, phrasing, and vocabulary.
- Punctuation is used with some degree of accuracy; spelling is either correct or phonetically consistent, and the writer may attempt to use difficult words.
- The paper is written in complete sentences.

3 points

- A "3" paper is solid but not outstanding; it shows some imagination, and the story holds the reader's interest; however, the paper is not "special."
- The writer gives details, and the paper contains more than a single idea; it has continuity—the paper holds together as a piece.
- The paper shows some good sentence structure but may have run-on sentences or incomplete sentence fragments; spelling is either correct or phonetically consistent.

2 points

- The paper expresses a single idea with some development; it has no personal or imaginative touch.
- The paper may not hold together, may ramble, or is too brief.
- The writer uses mostly simple sentences; spelling errors may be common, and phonetic spelling is inconsistent; there is little punctuation or intentional capitalization.

1 point

- The paper has a single idea.
- The paper is short and sparse with no imagination.
- Sentence structure is poor or lacking; phonetic spelling is inconsistent; there is little punctuation or intentional capitalization.

Grades 3 and 4

4 points

- The writer's genuine interest and involvement come across to the reader.
- The piece is imaginative, and the plot is well developed and shows continuity.

- The writing includes attention to detail and description; vocabulary may be interesting or specific.
- The paper has a minimum of mechanical errors.

3 points

- The writer has made some interest and involvement evident to the reader.
- The piece shows some imagination; plot is less complex and less developed than a "4" paper.
- The piece has some unity but is less interesting than a "4."
- The writer provides less detail and uses less intricate vocabulary than in a "4."

2 points

- The plot is not compelling; it has no development, and the piece is not interesting to readers.
- The piece shows little imagination.
- The writer gives little attention to detail or to vocabulary.
- The writing lacks complex sentence structures.

1 point

- The piece represents a single thought without development; it is trite and uninteresting, is short, and seems to reflect only minimal effort.

Grades 5 and 6

4 points

- The piece shows sustained effort.
- The writer sticks with a central theme and develops it; the paper is highly imaginative and interesting to read; it shows depth of feeling.
- The paper has a sense of wholeness; it has a beginning, middle, and end.
- The piece shows good use of expressive and descriptive vocabulary.
- Sentence structure is clear; punctuation and spelling are strong, with accurate grammar and usage.

3 points

- The piece shows some imagination and communicates some feeling.
- The sense of wholeness is not quite as strong as in a "4" paper.
- The piece shows some expressive and descriptive vocabulary.
- Spelling and punctuation are not always accurate.

2 points

- The writer's level of effort appears to have wavered.
- The piece is not convincing or interesting, is flat, and communicates little feeling; there is little sense of wholeness or continuity.
- Sentence structure is quite simple, with many run-on sentences.

1 point

- The writer's effort seems minimal.
- The piece is flat, predictable, and undeveloped; it is unimaginative and does not communicate feeling.
- Syntax and spelling are very poor, with choppy, poorly punctuated sentences.

Grades 7 and 8

4 points

- Stories have a good plot; papers are organized and unified with a conclusion or resolution.
- Papers either are interesting or handle the subject in a unique way.
- Detail is effectively used.
- Blatant cliché is avoided.
- The writer has made few mechanical errors.

3 points

- Plot development is adequate; the paper has organization, is unified, and holds together as a piece; it has conclusion or resolution.
- The paper offers some interesting ideas but shows little imagination.
- Detail is used but is not enriching to the content.
- The writer has made several mechanical errors.

2 points

- The piece has a simple plot; the story is trite, with minimum imagination.
- Little detail is provided.
- The writer has made many mechanical errors.
- Contents and creativity may be similar to the "3" paper, but the higher number of language mechanics difficulties distinguish the "2" paper.

1 point

- The piece has no plot, lacks focus, and is poorly organized; minimum effort is suspected; absence of imagination makes the paper boring to read.
- Few or no details are given.
- The reader encounters so many mechanical errors that the content is difficult to read; sentence structure is very unsophisticated; the paper appears messy, looking much like an early draft.

Appendix B

Policy of the National Board for Professional Teaching

In this policy, the National Board presents its view of what teachers should know and be able to do. Its convictions about what it values and believes guide all of the National Board's standards and assessment processes.

The fundamental requirements for proficient teaching are relatively clear: a broad ground in the liberal arts and sciences; and knowledge of the subjects to be taught, the skills to be developed, and the curricular arrangements and materials that organize and embody that content. Requirements also include knowledge of general and subject-specific methods for teaching and for evaluating student learning; knowledge of students and human development; skills in effectively teaching students from racially, ethnically, and socioeconomically diverse backgrounds; and the skills, capacities, and dispositions to employ such knowledge wisely in the interest of students.

This enumeration suggests the broad base for expertise in teaching but conceals the complexities, uncertainties and dilemmas of the work. The formal knowledge teachers rely on accumulates steadily, yet provides insufficient guidance in many situations. Teaching ultimately requires judgment, improvisation, and conversation about means and ends. Human qualities, expert knowledge and skill, and professional commitment together compose excellence in this craft.

The National Board has led the vanguard effort to develop professional standards for elementary and secondary school teaching. The National Board Certified Teachers stand for professionalism in the schools. The National Board's responsibility is not only to ensure that teachers who become National Board Certified meet its professional standards of commitment and competence, but also to maintain standards and assessments that are so well regarded that America's accomplished teachers will decide to seek National Board Certification.

Policy Position (Five Core Propositions)

The National Board for Professional Teaching Standards seeks to identify and recognize teachers who effectively enhance student learning and demonstrate the high level of knowledge, skills, abilities, and commitments reflected in the following five core propositions.

1. Teachers are committed to students and their learning.

Accomplished teachers are dedicated to making knowledge accessible to all students. They act on the belief that all students can learn. They treat students equitably, recognizing the individual differences that distinguish one student from another. In their practice, they take these differences into account. They adjust their practice based on observation and knowledge of their students' interests, abilities, skills, knowledge, family circumstances, and peer relationships.

Accomplished teachers understand how students develop and learn. They incorporate the prevailing theories of cognition and intelligence in their practice. They are aware of the influence of context and culture on behavior. They develop students' cognitive capacity and their respect for learning.

Equally important, they foster students' self-esteem, motivation, character, civic responsibility, and their respect for individual, cultural, religious, and racial differences.

*2. Teachers know the subjects they teach
and how to teach those subjects to students.*

Accomplished teachers have a rich understanding of the subject(s) they teach and appreciate how knowledge in their subject is created, organized, linked to other disciplines, and applied to real-world settings. While faithfully representing the collective wisdom of our culture and upholding the value of disciplinary knowledge, they also develop the critical and analytical capacities of their students.

Accomplished teachers command specialized knowledge of how to convey and reveal subject matter to students. They are aware of the preconceptions and background knowledge that students typically bring to each subject and of strategies and instructional materials that can be of assistance. They understand where difficulties are likely to arise and modify their practice accordingly. Their instructional repertoire allows them to create multiple paths to the subjects they teach, and they are adept at teaching students how to pose and solve their own problems.

*3. Teachers are responsible for
managing and monitoring student learning.*

Accomplished teachers create, enrich, maintain, and alter instructional settings to capture and sustain the interest of their students and to make the most effective use of time. They also are adept at engaging students and adults to assist their teaching and at enlisting their colleagues' knowledge and expertise to complement their own. Accomplished teachers command a range of generic instructional techniques, know when each is appropriate, and can implement them as needed. They are as aware of ineffectual or damaging practice as they are devoted to elegant practice.

They know how to engage groups of students to ensure a disciplined learning environment and how to organize instruction to allow the schools' goals for students to be met. They are adept at setting norms for social interaction among students and between students and teachers. They understand how to motivate students to learn and how to maintain their interest even in the face of temporary failure.

Accomplished teachers can assess the progress of individual students as well as that of the class as a whole. They employ multiple methods for measuring student growth and understanding and can clearly explain student performance to parents.

4. Teachers think systematically about their practice and learn from experience.

Accomplished teachers are models of educated persons, exemplifying the virtues they seek to inspire in students—curiosity, tolerance, honesty, fairness, respect for diversity, and appreciation of cultural differences—and the capacities that are prerequisites for intellectual growth: the ability to reason and take multiple perspectives to be creative and take risks, and to adopt an experimental and problem-solving orientation.

Accomplished teachers draw on their knowledge of human development, subject matter and instruction. They also draw on their understanding of their students to make principled judgments about sound practice. Their decisions are grounded not only in the literature but also in their experience. They engage in lifelong learning, which they seek to encourage in their students.

Striving to strengthen their teaching, accomplished teachers critically examine their practice, seek to expand their repertoire, deepen their knowledge, sharpen their judgment and adapt their teaching to new findings, ideas, and theories.

5. Teachers are members of learning communities.

Accomplished teachers contribute to the effectiveness of the school by working collaboratively with other professionals on instructional policy, curriculum development, and staff development. They can evaluate school progress and the allocation of school resources in light of their understanding of state and local educational objectives. They are knowledgeable about specialized school and community resources that can be engaged for their students' benefit, and are skilled at employing such resources as needed.

Accomplished teachers find ways to work collaboratively and creatively with parents, engaging them productively in the work of the school.

What the National Board Will Value in Teaching

The rich amalgam of knowledge, skills, dispositions, and beliefs that will characterize National Board Certified teachers are clustered under the five core propositions presented above.

References

Ainsworth, L. (2003). *Power standards: Identifying the standards that matter most.* Englewood, CO: Advance Learning Press.

Arter, J. A., & McTighe, J. (2000). *Scoring rubrics in the classroom: Using performance criteria for assessing and improving student performance.* Thousand Oaks, CA: Corwin.

Ausubel, D. P. (2000). *The acquisition and retention of knowledge: A cognitive view.* Boston: Kluwer Academic.

Bloom, B. S. (1956). *Taxonomy of educational objectives: The classification of educational goals: Handbook 1: Cognitive domain.* New York: Longman.

Chapman, C., & King, R. (2003). *Differentiated instructional strategies for writing in the content areas.* Thousand Oaks, CA: Corwin.

Colachico, D. (1996). Unpublished course and workshop presentation materials on strategies for teaching special education pupils. Used by permission. (Contact author at dcolachico@apu.edu)

Cummins, J. (2001). *Language, power, and pedagogy.* Retrieved August 11, 2004, from http://www.iteachilearn.com/cummins/lpp.html

Ehrgott, R., & Luehe, F. W. (1984). *Target teaching.* Visalia, CA: Key Publications.

Eisner, E. (1985). *The educational imagination.* London: Collier McMillian.

Elliott, D., & Holtrop, S. (1999). *Nurturing and reflective teachers: A Christian approach for the 21st century.* Claremont, CA: Coalition of Christian Teacher Educators/Council for Christian Colleges and Universities (distributed through Learning Light Publishing).

Gannon, J. (2003). *Jan's thoughts and resources on classroom management.* Retrieved August 2, 2004, from http://www.geocities.com/janice13/community.html

Goldhaber, D., & Anthony, E. (2004, March 8). *Independent study confirms effectiveness of national board certification* (Center on Reinventing Public Education). Retrieved May 31, 2004, from http://www.crpe.org/workingpapers

Gordon, W. J. (1961). *Synectics.* New York: Harper & Row.

Gordon, W. J. (1977, April). Connection-making is universal. *Curriculum Product Review, 9*(4).

Greene, J. (1998). *A meta-analysis of the effectiveness of bilingual education* (Tomas Rivera Policy Institute, in collaboration with the University of Texas at Austin and Harvard University). Claremont, CA: Tomas Rivera Policy Institute.

Gunter, M. A., Estes, T. H., & Schwab, J. A. (1995). *Instruction: A models approach.* Boston: Allyn & Bacon.

Gunter, M. A., Estes, T. H., & Schwab, J. A. (2003). *Instruction: A models approach* (3rd ed.). Boston: Allyn & Bacon.

Guskey, T. (2003). *Guilderland Central School District grading policy.* Retrieved August 1, 2004, from http://www.guilderlandschools.org/district/General_Info/Grading.htm

Harrow, A. (1972). *A taxonomy of the psychomotor domain: A guide for developing behavioral objectives.* New York: David McKay.

Hunter, M. (1976). *Prescription for improved instruction.* El Segundo, CA: TIP Publications.

Hunter, M. (1989). *Mastery teaching.* El Segundo, CA: TIP Publications.

Jessness, J. (2004). *Teaching English language learners K-12: A quick-start guide for the new teacher.* Thousand Oaks, CA. Corwin Press.

Joyce, B., & Weil, M. (2000). *Models of teaching* (6th ed.). Englewood Cliffs, NJ: Prentice Hall.

Joyce, B., Weil, M., & Showers, B. (1991). *Models of teaching* (4th ed.). Boston: Allyn & Bacon.

Joyce, B., Weil, M., & Showers, B. (1995). *Models of teaching* (5th ed.). Boston: Allyn & Bacon.

Katayama, A. D., & Robinson, D. H. (2000, Winter). Getting students partially involved in note taking using graphic organizers. *The Journal of Experimental Education, 68*(2), 119–133.

Krashen, S. (2000). Bilingual education: Current challenges. *Educators for Urban Minorities, 1*(2), 53–68.

Krathwohl, D. R., Bloom, B. S., & Masia, B. B. (1964). *Taxonomy of educational objectives: The classification of educational goals. Handbook 2: Affective domain.* New York: Longman.

Lindsey, R. B., Robins, K. N., & Terrell, R. D. (2003). *Cultural proficiency: A manual for school leaders* (2nd ed). Thousand Oaks, CA: Corwin.

Marlington School District. (2003). *Grades and grading policy.* Retrieved August 1, 2004, from http://dukes.stark.k12.oh.us/grade.html

Marzano, R. J. (2001). *Designing a new taxonomy of educational objectives.* Thousand Oaks, CA: Corwin.

Moskal, B. M. (2003). Recommendations for developing classroom performance assessments and scoring rubrics. *Practical Assessment, Research & Evaluation, 8*(14). Retrieved August 1, 2004 from http://PAREonline.net/getvn.asp?v=8&n=14

National Council for Teachers of English. (2003). *Because writing matters.* Retrieved August 1, 2004, from http://www.writingproject.org/pub/nwpr/voice/2003n04/staff6.html

National Council for Teachers of Mathematics. (2003). *Principles and standards for school mathematics: An overview.* Retrieved August 1, 2004, from http://www.nctm.org/standards/standards.htm

National Writing Project. (2004). Home page. http://www.writingproject.org/ or email nwp@writingproject.org

National Board for Professional Teaching. (2003). Standards. Retrieved June 11, 2003, from http://www.nbpts.org/

Oliver, D., & Shaver, J. P. (1971). *Cases and controversy: A guide to teaching the public issues series.* Middletown, CT: American Education Publishers.

O'Neill, W. F. (1990). *Educational ideologies: Contemporary expressions of educational philosophy.* Dubuque, IA: Kendall/Hunt.

Palmer, P. J. (1993). *To know as we are known: Education as a spiritual journey.* San Francisco: Harper.

Palmer, P. J. (1997). *The courage to teach.* San Francisco: Harper.

Rogers, C. (1982). *Freedom to learn for the 80's.* Columbus, OH: Charles E. Merrill.

Serafini, B. L. (2000). *The Jersey Shore Area School District grading policy.* Retrieved August 1, 2004, from http://www.jsasd.k12.pa.us/bserafini/Grading%20Policy.htm

Slavin, R. E. (1995). *Cooperative learning: Theory, research, and practice.* Boston: Allyn & Bacon.

Taba, H. (1967). *Teacher's handbook for elementary social studies.* Reading MA: Addison Wesley.

U.S. Department of Education, Office of English Language Acquisition. (2004, January). *Declaration of rights for parents of English language learners.* Retrieved August 11, 2004 http://www.ed.gov/about/offices/list/oela/index.html?src=oc

Wiggins, G. (2002, January). *Grant Wiggins on assessment.* Retrieved August 13, 2004 (http://www.glef.org/php/interview.php?id=Art_935&key=005)

Index